# FIREFIGHTER INTERVIEW

# RULE BOOK

## FIRST EDITION

D1615811

Mike Zolin

&

Rob Christensen

Published By TopScore


Interview911.com Publications

Thanks to our editors:

Randy Barnack, Chris Ferguson, Tim Maxfield and Tina O'Rourke

This book is brought to you by TopScore and www.interview911.com

Testimonials:

Mike Zolin and Rob Christensen, I am writing today to let both of you know that the information and instruction that you gave is second to none. I have been offered positions with two different fire departments as a direct result of the high interview scores that I received. Before taking this class I was not adequately able to express the reasons that I should be hired to work as a firefighter. After your class I became confident during my interviews. I know it isn't magic. It's about learning how to express the deep desire you have to follow your calling and you taught me how to do it. I am certain that what you taught me would be good advice for those looking for any job from mechanic to CEO. Words are nice but the proof in is the pudding.

Following my last interview, one of the interviewers asked the others: "Does anyone else feel like standing up and clapping?"

**R. Pettinger**
**Valedictorian F.D.N.Y Spring 2002 Recruit Class**

My very first testing experience was with the largest department in the state. I somehow got lucky and passed the written test all on my own, so I decided I would prepare for the oral board on my own too. big mistake! I didn't have a clue what kind of questions the board would likely ask, and even if I did it wouldn't have mattered - I had no idea HOW to properly answer them! I was clueless of how the oral board process works, and needless to say, I did not get the job. Two years later the same department was testing again so I decided to get some help, and I'm so glad I did. After working with the guys at TopScore, my oral board score skyrocketed from an 80 to a 95! That test was the second test I had ever taken, and the only difference between my two testing experiences was the proper guidance and training I received at TopScore. The second time around I DID get the job, and now I'm working for my dream department. I know I would not be a firefighter here today if it weren't for TopScore!

**B. Skolvin**

**Summary**- There is a lot of information in this book. We will start with a brief summary on the most important things we will cover. Just keep them in mind: we will cover them in great detail later in the book.

There are two types of interview questions: *Real* and *What if*.

*Real*- These interview questions are exactly what they sound like. They are about you and your life experiences. You will learn how to answer **Real** questions using the *TopScore Top Five*. This is where you include five parts to make one complete answer.

*What if*- questions. These questions are fictional. There are three types of **what if** questions.

     1- Situational

     2- Leading

     3- Interpersonal

We will also cover over 70 must know **Rules** , **Core values** and your **Marketing Priorities**. During a Fire department interview, there are a number of important things you need to do and say. Probably more important, however, may be things you should not do or say. These important pieces of information are what we like to call *The Rules*.

Attaining a position as a professional firefighter is considered by many to be impossible. It is not uncommon to hear a fire department having 2,000 applicants for no more than 20 available positions. Quick math will tell you your initial odds could be as low as one percent. With these odds, it is clear why so many people call it impossible. For *TopScore* students, it is our goal as coaches to make it POSSIBLE!! Teaching people how to succeed in the firefighter interview is what we excel in. We believe it is because we have a passion for helping people. Sitting on numerous oral boards as well as coaching candidates has given us a great insight of the interview process. You will find that the *Firefighter Interview Rule Book* is unlike any other interview book available. This book will *not* give you answers to 101 different interview questions. If we answered all of the questions for you, the answers would be ours, not yours, and then everyone who read our book would give the same answers. What we do provide, however, are the tools to answer any question with a simple to understand five-step process for each question called the *TopScore Top Five*. The *TopScore Top Five* system is a framework that helps provide structure to answers on your next firefighter interview.

You will also learn how to incorporate your Core Values as well as your personalized Marketing Priorities into your *TopScore* answer. YOURURBANDICTIONARY.COM, January 2015 defines *Core Values* as the fundamental beliefs of a person or an organization. Core values are the guiding principles that dictate your behavior and actions.

*Marketing Priorities* are the highlights from your life. Marketing Priorities are the things you want the oral board to know about you. Some of these priorities can be gathered from your resume, but not all Marketing Priorities will be on a person's resume. For example, you may have a specific event when you were sixteen years old as the first person on location of a car accident. The accident resulted with one trauma patient who you were able to assist by stopping the bleeding and using first aid techniques you learned that year in health class. When the fire department arrived and took over the patient care, they complimented you on the great job you did and one of the firefighters mentioned an explorer program for teenagers with the fire department. It was from that day on that you knew you wanted to be a firefighter. We will talk more on both Core Values as well as Marketing Priorities later in the book.

With our past successes, we know this book has all the information you need to nail your interview. However, there is no way for us to know about every interview you could encounter. There are some interviews that can be different from the majority, so do your research before you start the process.

Why do we call our instructions a rule book? There are many rules to follow when testing for the fire department. Most if not all of these rules are not written anywhere, until now, but they do exist. We have established *The Rules* through years of interviews, coaching and feedback from our students. By not knowing *The Rules*, we have seen candidates fail without knowing it by saying just one wrong thing. We have learned what the oral board is looking for in a great answer. We are going to show you these previously hidden gems that will improve your score dramatically. Not knowing even one of the rules can be the difference between being hired or continuing on the testing circuit. We understand the time and expense that is involved in testing to become a firefighter; we have been there. Our goal is to help you cut down the amount of time, energy and expense involved in your pursuit of this amazing career. Our only caveat to your purchase of this book is the following: be dedicated to attaining your career and when you are hired, remain passionate for this great profession!

So you want to be a firefighter? Do you have what it takes? Employ the *TopScore* system and vault ahead of your competition on the way to earning your badge. The *TopScore* system utilizes a process of self-analysis to highlight your strengths and a process to deliver them to the oral board.

There are three major components in this book. They include the *TopScore Top Five*, the *TopScore Marketing Priorities* and the *Rules*. One of the great aspects of our book is that it is co-authored. This means it contains two different points of view and two different styles of teaching. One author's style of teaching is linear and the other is more creative. We were able to mesh them into this one-of-a-kind comprehensive book. Whatever the style that best suits you, we have it covered.

*TopScore's Top Five* are the foundation for answering questions and the *TopScore Marketing Priorities* are the polish to ensure you've not only answered the question, but have provided the oral board with enough information to really understand who you are and what you are capable of.

Included in this book are the rules you must learn before your first interview. By participating in numerous interviews and coaching for many years, we have learned the rules. The oral board members giving the interview know *The Rules*. So should you. You will see that parts of the interview are like playing a game. Knowing *The Rules* will help you be victorious in this game. The other key element to being victorious is having a great team. This is where the *TopScore* team comes in. Over the last fifteen years, our team of successful candidates continues to grow and grow. We are glad you picked us as part of your team. We have been down the path to victory and played the game many times. We are a family business that cares about helping people.

To truly grasp and implement the concepts discussed in this book, you will need to practice. Practice, and when you feel you have mastered the *TopScore* system, practice some more! Yes, this takes effort. A lot of effort, but nothing in life worth having is easy. If you need some motivation, find out when your local fire academy is holding a graduation and attend. You'll probably feel a little queasy as you watch the badges being pinned on the newest firefighters. That dose of envy needs to be refocused into motivation.

So let's get started- it's time to get to work!

**Getting Started**

**Rule: Do your research on the department.**

**Rule: Talk to the newest members to see what the department is looking for.**

Landing a position with a Fire Department is obviously a challenging process, so be prepared to step outside what is considered "normal" for a nine-to-five job. The process is extremely competitive. If you are a competitive person, embrace the process.

If you are not, you'll have to motivate yourself to become so. Remember: this is something you want!

Your first step to getting hired with a Fire Department is identifying which departments are hiring. There are subscription-based websites available that will post hiring notices for the areas you are interested in. The number of candidates hired and the frequency of hiring differs from department to department. Most of the larger departments will establish an eligibility list for their fire academies and draw from them as the need arises for additional firefighters. Other departments may hire individually; however, these departments might require a current firefighter and/or Emergency Medical Technician certification.

A department's website is an excellent resource for hiring information. Career interest cards and important hiring information can be accessed on the site and additional hiring resources may be available. Ensure that you are aware of any extra requirements needed to apply well in advance. The standard process for applying to be a new recruit in a Fire Department normally begins with submitting an interest card or registering, which then proceeds directly to a written test. Following the written test, a number of candidates will be eliminated. The remaining members then proceed to either a physical ability test or an oral interview (one follows the other no matter the order). Once these two hurdles are overcome, the candidates either go to a chief's interview or are rank-ordered according to their scores for hiring on an as needed basis. This rank order is usually held for a certain predetermined amount of time, and when this time has expired, the list is scrubbed and the whole process begins again. Some fire departments have their own training academies while others utilize outsourced academies which may be required to apply for an entry position. It behooves the applying member to check with his or her desired department to ascertain the prerequisites required for the job as well as the hiring process in general.

### Interest Cards

Some departments offer career interest cards as the first step in the hiring process. These cards are used to collect test candidates' contact information. Test candidates should treat the interest card as an invitation to apply.

### Written Test

The written test is used to cull the field and separate the wheat from the chaff. There are numerous written books and websites available for prospective candidates to utilize in preparing for a written test. Our advice is to contact the HR department of the fire department for which you are preparing to take the written test, and see if they have published the test format and/or which company is providing the test you will be taking.

A recent hiring at a local department at the time of this publishing brought in over 600 applicants for ten jobs. The previous hiring prior to this one brought in thousands. The reduced number of applicants during the second hiring resulted from a newly implemented requirement to be EMT certified. Yes, it's *that* competitive so study up!

### Physical Aptitude Test

The physical aptitude test is just what the name implies: physical. You will be required to conduct numerous physical maneuvers in a certain amount of time. This is most likely a pass/fail event. Once again, check with the local HR department to discover what is entailed in their physical assessment.

## Oral interview

Now we are getting into the bread and butter. If you have made it to an oral interview, you have distinguished yourself above many other candidates, but don't become complacent. This is where the true grit of a candidate is exposed, and it is fiercely competitive. Look for any and all opportunities to improve yourself. Remember: it could be a fraction of a percent separating someone from attaining his or her dream and others looking for the next test.

### The Oral Interview

Firefighters must be able to respond quickly and coordinate their activities as part of a highly effective team which is focused on attention to detail during stressful emergencies. They must have excellent communication skills and exercise compassion, dignity, and respect whether on the scene of an emergency, out with the public or back at the station.

At *TopScore,* we have always believed one of the greatest attributes of being a firefighter is our ability to show up at the scene of a fire and immediately go right to work. We don't have to pull the homeowner aside and advise them how fast we can pull the correct line, coordinate our fire attack with ventilation and prevent further damage to the structure. In other words, the homeowner completely trusts us to handle the situation without ever having us! There is no interview process and definitely no need to sell ourselves; we are simply expected to take care of the situation.

Unfortunately, however, landing the job will require you to become a great salesperson. You must accept and perfect the art of selling yourself. No one is going to shout out your accomplishments from the top of a mountain or campaign to the board about what a phenomenal asset you will be for the department. The most successful salespeople are individuals who wholeheartedly believe in the product they are selling. This means you need to believe, to your core, that you are the best investment for the department for whom you are testing. In essence, you are selling yourself. Who better to present an overwhelming positive view of your abilities and capabilities to the interview board? When you effectively sell yourself to the board, it will leave no doubt in their eyes you will be a tremendous asset, not only now, but 20 years into your career. Yes, this is uncomfortable for most individuals, and especially to those who are drawn to perform in the fire service. You must overcome these nagging doubts and prepare yourself to impart a convincing and outstanding presentation to the oral panel. It takes work, lots of work, but we can honestly say it's worth it!

The interview board will ask a wide range of questions with a specific objective. The board wants to get to know you to the best of their ability and to identify whether or not you will fit their department. The interview board is looking for more than just whether or not you're a person who is easy to get along with. They want to know if they can depend on you. They want to know whether they can trust you with their lives. You need to know and understand you are interviewing to be part of a family – their family. Always speak from your heart, stay positive and focus on your successes in life. You have only one sale that counts: You.

## Interview Preparation

Start by clearly identifying your goal. Write it down and post it where you will see it every day. Reading your goal and visualizing your success will help keep you motivated. You can't afford to be average. When people in need call on the fire department, they expect a brain surgeon who is a two-time Olympic athlete, and who can solve their problem in two seconds flat! They don't want someone average showing up at their door. Firefighters need to prepare for anything at any time. The public expects you to have the tools to answer their calls. Your interview panel shares the same mindset. They expect you to meet the objectives set forth in the questions they ask.

You are more marketable than you give yourself credit for. Often we do not give ourselves the respect and acknowledgement we deserve. In many cases, we are our own worst enemy. During an interview, do not downplay your experience, accomplishments or accreditations. For the candidate with very little work history and life experience, it is encouraged to dig through your past for any relevant experience for the job. The fact you delivered pizza for a summer can highlight that you are familiar with the city's address breaks, not to mention knowing fifty percent of the streets. Your mother is not going to be standing over your shoulder telling the board how wonderful her child is. You need to make it happen.

Obtaining a position with any fire department is a great challenge. Typically, there are several hundred or even several thousand candidates vying for a handful of positions. Think of this as a competition designed to separate the best from the best. However, as with any competition, there are rules. Fact: The students who are most prepared for their interview are the ones who perform the best.

14

**Learn the Job Description**

An important part of interview preparation is thoroughly knowing the department's job description. It is not only necessary to know the position you are testing for, but also critical to let the board know you clearly understand the expectations set before you. Do not allow T.V. shows or movies to be your impression of what a professional firefighter is. The majority of firefighter job descriptions are going to be similar no matter where you apply. Look for little, unique differences in the description and plan to bring them up in a positive way during your interview.

The following is an example from a small section of the Mesa Fire Department's job description. This was taken from the City of Mesa, Arizona's website in October 2013. Most departments' job descriptions will look something like this.

*Entry Level Mesa Firefighter Job Description*

*Overview: Firefighters must be able to respond quickly and coordinate their activities as an effective teamwork. This work requires attention to detail as well as skill in communication with compassion, dignity and respect.*

*Classification Responsibilities: Firefighters perform public safety work involving the protection of life and property by fighting fires, responding to emergency incidents, using*

Emergency Medical Services (EMS) skills, and engaging in fire code enforcement, public education, and station and equipment maintenance activities. This class is responsible for performing related duties as required.

*Distinguishing Features:* Upon successful completion of the Mesa Firefighter - Recruit Academy and completion of the criteria for promotion, Firefighter - Recruits are criteria -based promoted to the Firefighter classification. Firefighters are required to work 24-hour shifts and 56-hour work weeks, and may be assigned to work a day assignment (40-hour work week) while assisting on special projects. Work at the fire station and scenes of fires.

QUALIFICATIONS

*Minimum Qualification(s) Required.* Must meet the qualifications and special requirements for Firefighter Recruit. Must successfully complete the Mesa Firefighter -Recruit Training Academy and criteria for promotion to Firefighter. Possession of current State of Arizona Emergency Medical Technician (EMT) certification.

*Preferred/Desirable Qualification(s).* Coursework toward an Associate's Degree in Fire Science or Fire Science Technology from a regionally accredited college or university is preferred. Bilingual in Spanish is desirable.

*ESSENTIAL FUNCTIONS*

*Communication: Communicates with the general public and other City employees in performing community service and public education activities, conducting business inspections, presenting public safety training classes, participating in school programs, answering questions, delivering emergency care, and ensuring patient needs. Produces written documents to document technical and legal matters.*

*Manual/Physical:  Responds to emergency incidents, fights fires, and utilizes either basic life support (BLS) or advanced life support (ALS) and/or paramedic skills. Uses firefighting equipment, including fire hoses or apparatus at emergency incidents.  Assists in advancing hose lines and making hydrant connections. Operates the following:  hydraulic or pneumatic rescue equipment to rescue trapped or endangered persons and to force entry into locked vehicles or structures; fire apparatus during fire suppression activities. Uses axes, pry tools, and pike poles to enter vehicles or structures.  Uses common hand tools to overhaul a fire scene and perform routine fire apparatus maintenance duties.  Performs searches and rescues inside burning buildings.*

*Moves heavy objects (up to 185 pounds or more) including 5" fire hoses, EMS equipment, salvage equipment, smoke ejectors, trauma boxes and body boards for short distances (150 feet or less) with the assistance of an aid, in performing firefighting and related duties.*

*The duties listed above are intended only as general illustrations of the various types of work that may be performed. Specific statements of duties not included does not exclude them from the position if the work is similar, related, or a logical assignment to the position. Job descriptions are subject to change by the City as the needs of the City and requirements of the job change.*

As you can see, there are numerous details to the entry-level firefighter position. The more details in the job description, the more opportunities you have to showcase your similar qualifications and abilities. This particular job description emphasizes the arduous and at times heavy lifting a firefighter is required to perform. It would be beneficial to bring up your involvement in physical fitness activities and how you have been dedicated to a healthy and fit lifestyle. The document also states the candidate will be performing public training as well as speaking at public safety classes. Furthermore, they will be speaking to groups at fire-related school programs. This would be an instance when you want to highlight that you have performed in public speaking and that you have volunteered with children. If you have any experience with speaking Spanish, you would want to communicate this in your interview as well.

## Your First Impression

### Rule: Make a good first impression.

The oral board's first impression of you occurs well before you ever walk into the interview room. You are probably saying "What???" but that's right. Your application and resume' will provide the first impression, and (not to sound clichéd) no one gets a second chance to make a first impression. Your application and resume should highlight your skills and abilities in a manner that causes the oral board to form a positive view of you well before they ever meet you.

Applications these days are primarily completed online and submitted with the click of a button. They may or may not reach the oral panel, but they still need to be filled out properly. Have your application proofread before submitting it.

A resume, on the other hand, is reviewed by the oral panel and can either help or hurt you prior to your interview. The resume needs to be professional, one page, and should highlight your greatest assets. Make the best first impression you can prior to meeting the panel. Try to get your resume into your folder prior to your interview and print your resume on good quality paper. Imagine you are on the panel and you have seen 300 resumes, all on the same white, boring paper. Then you get a professional resume on quality paper. Is it going to stand out? Is it going to show effort and look better than any other resume? If they do not allow you to submit it early or you submitted a resume online, you should still bring in a few copies to give to the board. The copies you give them should be on high quality paper and look more professional than the ones given to them by Human Resources on plain computer paper.

**Second Impression** (Your first visible impression)

**Rule: Make a good impression.**

Your second impression begins the second you walk through the door for the interview. You need to enter the room with enthusiasm and confidence, look the panelists in the eyes, smile and give firm handshakes. A proper entry and introduction will get everything moving in the right direction. Do your best to remember their names and ranks. This will also help ensure that your follow-up thank you cards will reach the correct people.

Wait for a member of the oral board to invite you to take a seat. If the chair is twenty feet away from the table, you need to move it closer. Ask before doing it, and don't put it so close to the table that you invade the board members' personal space. Once seated, be aware of your body position and posture. You need to continue displaying confidence and respect. Simple body gestures such as placing your elbows on the table or slouching will send the wrong message. Studies show the spoken word accounts for approximately 8-35% of the message we are trying to convey (depending on the study referenced). This means that the remaining 65-92% percent is communicated non-verbally. Wow!

Amy Cuddy, a Social Psychologist and Associate Professor of Business Administration at Harvard Business School and keynote speaker on body language gave a talk at the June 2012 TED TALK Convention which is available on video. "Your body language shapes who you are," Amy stated. Amy spoke about how people are viewed by others and how they view themselves. She also hit on how to change others' perception of you. At time of this book's publication, the video had over 22-million views. Watch it now, and watch it again before your interview.


**Dress**

**Rule: Dress like a professional.**

It is simple; this is a job of professionals by professionals, so dress appropriately. Wear conservative business attire such as a dark colored suit with a white or gray shirt. A tie is a necessity for men. Women should wear knee-length skirts (or longer) or business suits/slacks with matching blouses. Neither gender should wear excessive jewelry. Avoid bright colors and distracting shirt or tie patterns. Remember: dress the part of a professional.

*The TopScore System*

There will be two types of questions during your interview: Real questions and What if questions.

*Real* questions deal with specific events and accomplishments you have accumulated throughout your life.  You will employ the *TopScore Top Five* with your *Marketing Priorities* and *Core Values* interwoven within your answer

*What if* questions deal with hypothetical situations. The oral board wants to judge your reaction and subsequent action to what are most likely uncomfortable situations.  *What if* questions will include Situational, Leading, and Interpersonal questions. The interview board will ask a wide range of questions with a specific objective. The board wants to get to know you to the best of their ability and to identify whether or not you will fit their department.

21

**Let's cover the *real* questions first.**

**Real questions.** You will answer using the *TopScore Top Five* approach:

Every answer will include:

1. Answer the question, and while answering the question, you will include the following in your answer:

2. Personal History (PH)      3-5 pieces

3. Personal Story (PS)      1- story

4. Department Knowledge (DK)   3-5 pieces

5. KeyWords (KW)      3-5 pieces

The 3-5 pieces are a guide line and usually make for a good sounding answer. You can have more than 5 but not less than 3.


## TopScore Top Five

**Rule: Utilize the *TopScore Top Five* to answer all Real questions.**


      Applying the *TopScore Top Five* is the approach to an answer which will garner a top score in the interview. The actual answer to the board's questions is only a small part of an excellent answer. The only reason the interview board is asking the question is to engage you and to judge your eagerness, ability and suitability from the answer you provide. ***Important items you add to support your answers are what will get you hired.*** Remember, there are five parts to a great answer: Answer the Question, add in some

**Personal History**, tell them a related **Personal Story**, show **Department Knowledge** and use **Key Words**. Add each of these into your response, and you'll have a strong answer that will set you apart from the competition.

To truly grasp and implement the concepts discussed in this book, you will need to practice and practice, and when you have done that, practice some more! Practice with people with whom you are less comfortable. This will help you to perform in the nerve-racking environment of the oral board. Practice in front of the mirror, while videoing yourself and in front of people. Most likely, the people you'll have access to and are willing to listen to you practice will not be firefighters, so plan on providing them with a checklist of things to look for. The *TopScore* Practice Interview Scorecard accomplishes this. Practicing your interview will ensure you are able to incorporate the topics discussed in this book and identify weak areas of your interview in time for them to be corrected.

Understanding and implementing the *TopScore Top Five* will guide you during your interview and set you apart from your competition. Your new-found confidence will give you momentum throughout the interview. These are the five things you need in every answer to a *Real* question. Most interviews are about thirty minutes long during which time you will have between four and eight *Real* questions. This time accounts for interviewees to elaborate on their answers by using the *TopScore Top Five*. The people who simply provide a basic answer will be finished with their interview in five minutes. Most people provide black and white answers to the questions asked of them, so the board will learn very little about them or about what they know about the department. For example, if there are eight questions, and you reply with five pieces of your personal history in every answer, the board will know forty more things about you! This will make their decision to hire you a lot easier. Thirty minutes is not a lot of time to get to know somebody who you are going to spend the next 25-years with. Think of the things you would want to know if you were getting married (spending the next 25-years with someone) and you had 3000 applicants who each had thirty minutes to answer your questions. You would pick the ones that gave you the most information about themselves (Personal History), spoke your language (KeyWords), who were able to tell you stories you will not forget (Personal Story) and who included why they would be a perfect fit based on their expert knowledge of you (Department Knowledge). Give the oral board the information they want to hear.

To reiterate, the *TopScore Top Five* approach applies only to the *Real* questions about you and your answer should include:

1. The Answer to the Question

2. Personal History (PH)          3-5 pieces

3. Personal Story   (PS)          1

4. Department Knowledge   (DK)    3-5 pieces

5. Key Words   (KW)               3-5 pieces

## #1= Answer the Question

> **Rule: Answer the question, the whole question. This might seem obvious, but part of the answer can often be missed. Some questions are multiple part questions in which interviewees fail to answer all parts of the question.**

For example

> Question: *What is the most important trait a firefighter must have and why?*

This is an example of a two-part question which needs two complete answers. You also need to incorporate the *TopScore Top Five* answer which includes Personal History, Personal Story(-ies), Department Knowledge and Key Words.

> Answer: *I believe the most important trait a firefighter must have is* (KW) *integrity. It is the very foundation of who firefighters are. I believe it is the trait or value, which defines our character. I know if you have* (KW) *integrity, you are committed to being* (KW) *honest,* (KW) *dependable,* (KW) *respectful and* (KW) *trustworthy.* (DK) *I see how your firefighters* (KW) *exemplify this trait and are* (KW) *dedicated to themselves, their crew, their community and their department. I know this because I have done numerous ride-alongs with your department. I have seen the* (KW) (DK) *integrity and work ethic of the firefighters and the attitude of the department. I was excited to see how* (KW) *progressive this department is. I learned about things your department has to offer such as* (DK) *Dive,* (DK) *Haz-Mat,* (DK) *Rope,* (DK) *Aircraft Rescue teams and a* (DK) *paramedic*

25

program with half of your (DK) *twenty-five stations being advanced life support engines covering* (DK) *300 square miles and* (DK) *30,000 calls per year. I know that when I see the* (KW) *dedication your members have for this department, it would make me proud to be a part of it.*

Integrity is most important because firefighters are entrusted with people's most prized possessions everyday. Whether those possessions are the lives of their family members and pets or home and personal belongings, firefighters embody a (KW) *trustworthy trait the community, our customers, depend on.* We do not have the option of betraying someone's trust. We are firefighters at all times, whether we are on or off duty.

I am (PH) *twenty nine years old with a* (PH) *wife and* (PH) *two young kids.* I grew up playing team sports like (PH) *football and* (PH) *hockey.* I am now in the (PH) *construction and remodeling business and often find myself with keys and codes to people's homes.* I do not take this responsibility lightly. (PS) *The success of my business rides not only on customer satisfaction once the project is complete but also how I treated them and their home.* (PS) *A customer may be happy with the outcome of the project, but if they do not trust me or like me as a person, they will never refer me to a friend.* My business depends on those referrals. I can tell you this: there is nothing in anyone's home that is worth the price of my integrity. More than anything, stealing and dishonesty are not in my genetic make-up.

(PS) *Just the other day, I was at one of the local box stores returning a few small items that I did not use on my last remodel. When I handed the cashier the items to scan and*

26

*return, she told me that they were not on my receipt. I then handed her the debit card I used to purchase the items, and again, she said the items were not purchased on that card. Without proof, the cashier could not give me cash, but would have to give me in-store credit instead. She began to set up a gift card for the balance and then it dawned on me: I had the correct receipt and the correct card. I double checked the receipt and realized that I was never charged. I had purchased several items at the same time, and somehow, four items were never scanned. I explained that I had purchased four identical items and had used two, but wanted to return the other two. She asked me what I wanted to do. I told her that I could not only decline the gift card, but I needed to be charged for the two items I used but did not pay for.*

*I live the (KW) value of (KW) integrity every day of my life, and I understand the importance it plays in life, business and especially the fire department. I know I can be counted on to continue the (DK) tradition of (KW) honesty, (KW) integrity and (KW) trustworthiness of this fire department.*

We highly recommend that you restate a multiple-part question back to the board. This gives you the opportunity to let yourself hear what it is you need to cover. It also provides for good two-way communication. There is also no problem with asking the board to repeat the question to be sure you heard all parts of it.

For Example

Question: *Tell the board a time when you faced a challenge in life in which you learned a valuable lesson and how it affected you as a person.*

You would repeat: *A time I faced a challenge in which I learned a valuable lesson and how I was affected was...,* and then continue with the *TopScore Top Five.*

*The TopScore Top Five* will greatly aid you because it provides structure to your response and will prevent rambling. When you have hit all five parts of your answer, you are done! The hardest part is learning how to segue from one part of your answer to the other to make it sound natural and fluid. The *TopScore Top Five* do not necessarily need to be addressed in any particular order, but each of these aspects must be addressed to receive a top score for your answer.

### #2=Personal History

#### Rule: Get your fishing lines in the water.

This is **your** history that consists of particular things the oral board will want to hear. For example, such things as where you were born, where you grew up, schools you attended, degrees you earned, your family, certifications and achievements as well as your hobbies, sports, trades and job history. Think of each piece of personal history as tags and titles you have accomplished throughout your life: student, son/daughter, waiter, soccer player, volunteer, etc. The more fishing lines you put in the water, the better your chances of hooking something. Hooking something is equivalent to getting an oral board member to associate with you. This is the first step in building any relationship. If you talk about things the board can relate to, they will naturally form a bond and view you as a likely candidate to hire.

For example:

*Growing up as the son of a firefighter, I was always interested listening to what my father would tell me when he came home from his shift at the firehouse. The stories that had me most interested were stories of how he was able to help someone during their time of need. With my young mind, I often viewed my father in the light of a superhero. These were my first memorable exposures to the job of a firefighter; little did I know that my father's stories planted the seeds for the career path that I would choose to pursue.*

Salesmanship requires you to show your enthusiasm, passion, positive attitude and compassion. Stay away from being negative or from showing political or religious opinions or prejudices. The art of salesmanship is building and cultivating relationships. When this happens, connecting those "personal history" fishing lines to the members on the board becomes natural, and you are guaranteed to have a more favorable score. The more lines in the water, the better your chances of catching something.

This is a real life example of relating to the oral board. A friend and I went to an interview at a local fire department. We had just graduated first (Me) and second (Jeff) in our college fire academy. Going into this interview, I thought I had it in the bag. I just knew I was going to score higher than Jeff. While talking after the interview, I expressed how well I felt I had done. Jeff said his interview was a bit different. The interview was going as expected, and then he mentioned he had a 1965 Mustang that he just finished restoring. As chance would have it, one of the captains across the table had the exact same Mustang. They spent the rest of the interview talking about their cars, where to get parts for their cars and trading technical tips. Guess who got the job? That's right, Jeff!

You never know to what the members of the oral board will relate. Simply stated, if they can relate to you, it is much easier for them to picture you as the ideal firefighter they desire to have as part of their team. It is easier to work with people who share common interests with you. Get those fishing lines in the water!

Homework- Write down your top 30 or more things you want the board to know about you. Your Personal History (PH)

1.

2.

3.

4.

5.

6.

7.

8.

9.

10.

11.

12

13.

14.

15.

16.

17.

18.

19.

20.

21.

22.

23.

24.

25.

26.

27.

28.

29.

30.

**: Employ stories they will remember.**

Think of your Personal History as the words and your Personal Story as the action.

You need to stand out to the oral board, and a solid Personal Story is imperative for this to happen. The Personal Story you choose to tell should support what you shared in your Personal History.  Anyone can boast about his/her excellent leadership qualities, but few can demonstrate them. Talk is cheap and actions speak louder than words.  It needs to be clear to the oral board that you are providing a personal story that actually happened and that supports what you described within your personal history. If you talk about being a good leader, you should have a good Personal Story to back it up.  It will usually start with something like "One time I…" or "I remember when I…" This is where you will employ your *Marketing Strategies* interlaced with *Core Competencies*. We will cover these later in the book, and they will help you narrow down some of your valuable stories.

Question: *Explain to the Board what you consider as a personal weakness.*

Answer: *Public speaking is an area I am working to improve. Sitting here in front of you reminds me of a feeling I had before a speech I gave in the fifth grade. (PS) I was running for (PH) student body vice president, and I stood in front of my entire grade school to give my speech, when I completely froze. The kids started to giggle and I stepped away from the podium to gather myself before I tried again. This happened about three times before the principal finally leaned in behind me and whispered, "Why don't you start with your* name?" With that suggestion, my speech came back to me. I stepped up to the microphone and (KW) *delivered. (PH) As it turned out, I won the election. I guess it's mostly about being memorable when you're in elementary school.*

*Since then, I've gotten a lot more comfortable speaking in front of people, but, in that moment while I was figuring out public speaking in elementary school, at the back of the auditorium stood both my parents supporting me, just as they had while I practiced the speech over and over. I do not consider my public speaking a strength, but I can assure you it is better than it used to be.*

*I know Backdraft Fire Department has been teaching (DK) Fire Safety since the early 1930's. (DK) Teaching 25 first and second graders about Stop Drop and Roll is something to which I am truly looking forward. I mentioned that my (PH) parents have encouraged me back in fifth grade. They continue to do so as they did on the phone this morning prior this interview. (KW) Following their example, encouraging others has become second nature for me. I enjoy helping people (KW) succeed.*

## #4= Department Knowledge

**Rule: Look on the internet for useful information about the department with who you are testing. Do ride-alongs to find crucial information not available on the web.**

Of course you want to be a firefighter, but why do you want to be a firefighter with this particular department? Department knowledge showcases your interest in the department you are interviewing for – their department! Firefighters who work, live, breathe, sweat and bleed together have a tremendous amount of pride and appreciation for what their department accomplishes on a daily basis.

Showing ample department knowledge accomplishes two things. First, it demonstrates interest in and commitment to your future department. It proves that you've embraced the challenge and you take your future job seriously; it shows sincerity and a commitment to be a part of the department. Second, it will help to ensure that you've selected the department best suited for you. Talk about the department's strategic plan and include the department's mission statement in your answers.

For example: *"I believe in Backdraft Fire Department's mission statement. It states "…". Therefore, I would "…".*

A way to learn the specifics about a department is to schedule a ride-along. Ride-alongs are extremely important for gaining information regarding the department to which you are applying. Schedule them. If the department you are applying to does not allow ride-alongs, make it a point to visit several different stations with cookies, ice cream, a list of *TopScore* questions and a fantastic attitude.

General fire history is also important to master. You need to become a student of all aspects of the profession. Learn who started the fire service and why. What is the Maltese Cross and how did it become the badge of the fire service? Why are fire trucks painted red? How and why did fire poles come about? Learn the facts and figures about the fire department to which you are applying, as well as the fire service in general, and you will give yourself one more edge over the competition.

Homework- Write down 20 significant facts regarding the fire department you are testing for. These will be found online and during your ride alongs.

1.                                             11.

2.                                             12.

3.                                             13.

4.                                             14.

5.                                             15.

6.                                             16.

7.                                             17.

8.                                             18.

9.                                             19.

10.                                            20.

## #5= Key Words

**Rule: Use Key Words, especially words popular with their department.**

*Key Words* are terms a fire department holds in high esteem. They can be found in a department's mission statement, strategic plan and recruitment guidelines. You should utilize these important *Key Words* to highlight your experience and accomplishments. These *Key Words* are so important, you shouldn't be surprised to see the oral board members make notes each time you use one in your answer.

For example: you are asked a simple question such as *"What is your favorite color?"*

If you simply answer "blue," you will not get hired.

You need to give the board enough information to understand why you chose blue..

Instead, answer:

*My favorite color is blue. Blue has been my favorite color as long as I can remember. My first (PH) hockey jersey was a blue Hartford Whalers jersey. Playing with the Whalers was how I learned the value of the (KW) teamwork and (KW) camaraderie associated with being part of a winning team. My friends and I were not the best players in the league, but we played as a team. We worked together towards the same goal, and we managed to win the (PH) championship in 2008. (PS) I can still remember the great feeling of skating around and passing the trophy from teammate to teammate, plus the fun we had at the celebration afterward. I have played team sports my entire life. I grew up playing*

*(PH) soccer and then transitioned to (PH) football and eventually (PH) ice hockey. I know the Fire Department is one big team that gains from the (KW) strength of all involved. Working as a team can be (KW) safer, faster and more enjoyable than working alone. I know from my ride-alongs that your fire department has many teams. They include (DK) four person engine and (DK) six person truck companies. You also have (DK) Dive, (DK) Tech, (DK) Haz-Mat and (DK) Aircraft Rescue Firefighting teams. I would be honored to be part of this (KW) progressive department, and I look forward to joining one of your specialty teams in the future.*

Despite the simplicity of the question about your favorite color, good use of *Key Words* along with the rest of the *TopScore Top Five* will tell the oral board exactly what they need to know about you. The sample answer above told the board several things. The board now knows that you play hockey, you work well in a team environment, you enjoy the camaraderie of working together and that you are able to obtain goals through synergy. The board learned all of this by simply listening to you explain why your favorite color is blue.

Remember: *Key Words* are simply another segue to an opportunity to tell the board more about you. Each keyword must have substance behind it. The last thing the board wants to hear when they ask "What is your favorite color?" is a canned answer. You need to always involve all aspects of the *TopScore Top Five* into your answer. Remember to find out what *Key Words* are important to the departments to which you are applying.

**Examples of a *Real* question:**

**Rule: Answer *Real* questions using the *TopScore Top Five* approach.**

*Real* questions will probably be asked first. Odds are, you will be asked a question similar to "Tell us about yourself." This is a *Real* question and an icebreaker. Below are examples of *Real* questions and possible answers. Remember, the suggestions provided should give you a good idea of where to start your answer. All aspects of the *TopScore Top Five* must be incorporated in your response.

Question: *What impact does stress and pressure have on a person's decision-making skills?*

Answer: *Stress and pressure will stimulate a person in one of two ways: negatively or positively. Negative stimulation will result in a poor decision or can lead to quick decisions, both resulting in mistakes or compromising (KW) safety. As a high school student in California, I played team sports. They included (PH) soccer, (PH) hockey, (PH) track and (PH) swimming. I learned a great deal about (KW) teamwork, (KW) camaraderie and (KW) leadership. One night I also learned about peer pressure. (PS) One of my friends from the varsity soccer team talked me into sneaking out for the night to toilet paper another teammate's home. I knew if I was caught, I would have to answer to my disappointed parents as well as my friend's parents, but I didn't want to be a considered a wimp. I wanted to be considered one of "the gang", so I gave in. Sure enough, I was caught by my dad. I then had to approach my friend's parents and confess to the toilet paper job.*

(PS) *A positive reaction can make certain people more efficient. When people are trained to operate during times of high stress and are equipped with the proper tools for the job, their* (KW) *situational awareness is high.* (DK) *Here at Backdraft Fire Department, the training department is recognized as one of the best in the state.* (DK) *Backdraft Fire Department recognizes and makes training a high priority within their department. More importantly, you train members to learn how to deal with and work in stressful situations.*

(PS) *Last summer, while dining at a local restaurant, a gentleman who was sitting a few tables away from me suffered a major heart attack. A person nearby witnessed the event and rushed over to the unconscious man and started a quick assessment. He then told a customer to call 9-1-1. Little did I know, the* (PH) *CPR training I completed five years earlier during my senior year of high school was about to be put to the test. I sprang from my chair without hesitation and assisted the bystander with moving the patient to the floor. The bystander asked me if I knew C.P.R. and I responded, "Yes, I do". He told me to perform chest compressions. I kneeled beside the patient and without even thinking I located the notch where the lower part of the rib meets the center of the chest and began counting as I compressed the patient's chest. I continued compressions for five minutes until the fire department arrived on scene. Obviously, this went from a calm night having dinner to a very significant and stressful event. That evening I learned a lot about how I would respond in a stressful situation. I had previous training, albeit five years prior, and despite the passage of time, I had perfect memory recall and was able to stay focused and calm while performing CPR.*

Let's examine the response above to see what aspects of the *TopScore Top Five* were addressed.

Answer the Question—The question was answered and a positive spin was put on it.

Personal History – High school athlete, varsity soccer, hockey, track and swimming, family.

Personal Story – Peer pressure.

Key Words – *Team, teamwork, camaraderie and leadership.*

Department knowledge – Talking about the training department being recognized as one of the best in the state demonstrates you have studied this specific department.

QUESTION: *We know what you can offer the Backdraft Fire department, but what can the Backdraft Fire Department offer you?*

ANSWER: *Working for this fire department can offer me (KW) security, (KW) camaraderie and a true sense of (KW) accomplishment. Your (DK) training department is well-respected amongst neighboring departments. This department also has the best (DK) personal protective equipment on the market for its members, (KW) progressive training that includes (DK) RIT, (DK) EMS, plus many specialty teams such as (DK) Dive, (DK) Rope, (DK) Aircraft Rescue Firefighting and (DK) Hazardous Materials. (PS) During my senior year of high school, I was honored to be the (PH) captain of the (PH) football team as well as the (PH) baseball team. (PS) I can still remember the honor I felt when my coach said he choose me to be captain because, day in and day out, I always brought my best. (PS) The single, most important lesson my coaches provided me for my success was to set clear expectations. Clear expectations as a captain of the team included but were not limited to my general conduct, my (KW) positive attitude, my (KW) work ethic and the level of skill I was to deliver on the field. The expectations that placed on me were all I needed to bring my very best day-in and day-out. If I did not mention before, I am extremely competitive. (PS) It is my competitive nature to exceed any standard set before me. (DK) I have read Backdraft Fire Department's Standards, Mission Statement and Vision Statement. I clearly understand what is expected of me by this department, regardless of whether I am working at the scene of an emergency, around the station or demonstrating specific proficiencies.*

Let's examine the response above to see what aspects of the TopScore Top5 were addressed.

Answer the Question – Again, the question was answered. The department offers me security and safety in the best personal protective equipment with the best available training. They offer an opportunity to be a part of their specialty teams. TopScore provides clear expectations from the guiding documents such as Mission and Vision statements.

Personal History – California, High school, football and baseball. Captain of both teams

Personal Story – Promoted to captain. Competitive Nature to exceed standards.

Keywords – *Respected, progressive, safe, camaraderie, positive attitude, work ethic*

Department knowledge –Know department members receive the best PPE training including Rapid Intervention Teams, Emergency Medical Service and the following specialty teams: Dive, Technical Rescue, Aircraft Rescue Firefighting and Hazardous Materials. Showed knowledge of the Standards and the Mission Statement.

Question: *Describe a time when you were faced with change. How did you react?*

Answer: *Change equals stress. Some people allow stress to control their actions, and others have a way of embracing stress/change. I learned to embrace stress as a* (KW) *motivator to accomplish the tasks I had in front of me. Some people might let stress control their lives and slow or halt their progress. If you look at it as a threat or problem instead of an opportunity, it will control you. When I graduated from* (PH) *college with a* (PH) *4.0 GPA and an* (PH) *A.S. degree in fire science, a part of me didn't want to leave the area I lived in because of the* (KW) *family,* (KW) *camaraderie and service I experienced as part of my* (PH) *fraternity. Even though my life was about to experience a big change, I knew it was time for me move on and put my life experiences to work. I was able to make many new friends at school as well as a* (PH) *volunteer for the local Boys and Girls Club. I know family and* (KW) *public service are important in the fire service, so much so that service is one of the three words on the Backdraft (DK) Department shield. In college each semester, we were required to do a minimal amount of community service. (PS) I consistently exceeded that number and posted the highest number of service hours for two consecutive semesters. I mentioned earlier that some look at stress as a problem, while others look at it as an opportunity. During 2013 Backdraft Fire Department responded (DK) 3,943 times to a variety of problems including (DK) 3,000 medicals, (DK) 300 fires, (DK) 30 extrications and many others. To me, this means Backdraft had close to 4,000 opportunities to provide exceptional customer service. I look forward to building future relationships and serving the community with this fire department.*

Let's examine the response above to see what aspects of the *TopScore Top Five* were addressed.

Answer the Question—This was a two-part question and both parts were addressed. The Change was that the candidate moved away from everything he/she had known. He/she moved far away from family and friends and embraced the change because it provided motivation to immediately make new friends at school as well as being a part of the community as a volunteer.

Personal History – The interview board now knows you graduated from college with a 4.0 GPA and an A.S. degree, were a member of a fraternity and enjoy building relationships.

Personal Story – The interview board knows you excel at public service.

Keywords – *family, camaraderie, motivation* and *service* were all addressed.

Department knowledge – The board knows you value the same things they do as represented on their department shield. You also mentioned the department's activities: 4,000 calls a year, 3,000 medicals, 300 fires and 30 extrications.

The **"*What If*"** Questions

> **Rule: Remember, these are make believe.**

> **Rule: Steer the oral board members in the direction you want them to go.**

Leave the board members in the make-believe world. Do *not* add personal stories or personal history. Some *Key Words* and *Department Knowledge* may be appropriate but are not required because they are in the *Real* questions. Don't rush through these questions; even if you have heard the question before and already know exactly what you are going to say, slow down and act as though you have never heard it before. Rushing a question might cause you to leave out information that could separate you from the other candidates.

*What if* questions include:

1. Leading

2. Situational

3. Interpersonal

Leading questions

Example: While on scene of a medical call, you see a fellow Firefighter pick up a twenty-dollar bill from the kitchen floor.

**Rule: Don't assume there is a problem.  Only assume positive.** By assuming negative, you may be viewed as being angry. By assuming positive, you assume that the other firefighters you work with are professional, trustworthy and acting in the best interest of the fire department.

You could start by saying: Firefighters are known for being honest and trustworthy. I would assume that it just fell out of his pocket.


## Rule: Defuse the bomb

Leading questions are attempting to lead you into assuming something negative. This is crucial to understand: leading questions are designed to make you assume that something negative is happening, and if you do, you will fail the question. When the board asks you a leading question, it's akin to them lighting the fuse to a bomb. If you know how to diffuse it or direct it in a better direction, you will be successful. There are a wide range of topics including theft, drinking and drug use.

Example #1

Question: *You see your captain drinking from a flask. What are you going to do?*

At this point, the fuse is lit. You attempt to defuse the bomb.

Response: *Yeah, we bought that for him for his birthday; it's our running joke, he keeps water in it.*

Now, the bomb is diffused. The board will not let you get away that easy, but they now know you understand the game. The board will then add,

Board: *You smell alcohol on his breath.*

You should continue to assume the positive.

Response: *This is a job of professionals. If I have to trust him with my life, I can trust that he is not drinking on the job. There are other things that could cause his breath to smell of alcohol like cold medicine or mouthwash. I don't think there is a problem.*

The board will then give you enough information to show you that something *is* wrong. In this situation, the person in question is undoubtedly drinking on the job. It is then your responsibility to correct the problem, taking it up the chain of command beginning at the lowest level and continuing until an acceptable outcome is obtained.

Board: *The Captain is also your father-in-law and is retiring in six months. You know if he is terminated, he will be left with no retirement!*

Your follow up on these types of answers must continue to reflect integrity, honor and devotion to the fire service.

Response: *I would inform the Captain that it is my obligation to report him to his supervisor since drinking on the job not only poses serious consequences to the firefighter in question, but also to his crew and the citizens we are entrusted to protect. I would also make myself available to accompany him to provide support and encouragement during this difficult time. It is the very least I could do, family member or not.*

By not immediately assuming anything was wrong, you diffused the bomb and formulated a *TopScore* answer which will gain the maximum points available for the question.

Example #2

> Question: *You see a fellow firefighter taking money out of the cash jar in the soda refrigerator, what do you do?*

Firefighting is a job of professionals by professionals. Since this is true, you should assume a positive outlook to the question. Don't initially assume the worst possible situation and make certain you take the time to craft an appropriate answer to the question.

An example approach could be that your fellow firefighter probably put a larger bill in the cash jar earlier and was now just making change for it. The interview board might continue the question by adding to the circumstances of the event. Stay positive and only positive until they provide enough information to prove that the firefighter was actually stealing. By staying with positive responses, you can control the direction of your answers. If they provide enough information to prove guilt and if what the firefighter in the question was doing is not legal, you must make sure the issue is addressed and is prosecuted to the fullest extent of the law. You owe it to your department and your profession to do so. Remember, this is a job of professionals by professionals and there is no room for illegal behavior.

> Response: *This is a job of professionals; we need to uphold the public's trust. We are responsible with their lives as well as their property. I should be able to trust my fellow firefighters with my life; surely I can trust him to get change from a jar on the soda refrigerator.*

Notice in the response above that only a positive outcome was assumed. As mentioned earlier, the board might pursue the situation and add to the circumstances of the situation.

Board: *There has been a lot of money missing.*

Response: I would make a note of it in my head, but I don't have any proof there is an actual problem. I would trust that that firefighter is doing the right thing until I have PROOF to the contrary.

You still have the opportunity to assume positive. Because you trust your fellow firefighters, you can trust they will pay it back. At some point in time, the board might state there is actual theft happening. At this point, you too must acknowledge the illegal behavior. You must address the problem and do whatever it takes to rectify the situation using the Chain of Command. The Chain of Command process provides the opportunity to deal with any situation at the lowest level possible.

Be prepared to explain how you will address and correct the problem. This piece of the question could be just as important as addressing the leading aspect of the question. When formulating your response, keep in mind the fire department is a family and the age-old rule of "treat others as you want to be treated," would apply. You should start by privately and respectfully addressing the issue with the firefighter in question. Wouldn't you expect the same respect from them? Perhaps you'll discover a personal issue provoking this behavior. Obviously, regardless of the problem, it's still not acceptable, but it shows compassion and respect and it presents an opportunity for them to rectify the situation before it escalates. This would be an uncomfortable situation, but inform the firefighter in question that he needs to speak with the Captain or Lieutenant (depending on your department), and you can offer to go with them. If the Captain does not address the situation, take it up the chain to the next highest rank. If the issue is still resolved, keep going up the chain. You know this is not acceptable behavior and it needs to be stopped. Remember, this is more than just a petty theft from a soda jar at the station. Each firefighter is an ambassador of the department and is trusted with the property of taxpayers. Can you imagine the damage to the department's reputation if a firefighter stole from someone they were entrusted to help?

**Situational Questions**

> **Rule: Pick a path and stick to it (stick to your guns).**

> **Rule: Use the Life Safety Order to justify your answer: your safety first, your crew's second, the public third and property fourth.**

> **Rule: Risk a lot to save a lot and risk a little to save a little (or what is already lost).**

> **Rule: Try to give them another option. This demonstrates critical thinking.**

> **Rule: Be confident in your answer. The board will be tougher on you if you are unsure.**

Situational questions are designed to make you change your mind. You need to pick a path, justify why you chose it and stick to the path you picked. From the limited info given, either path is correct. Make sure you justify why you picked the path you did. The interview board will make the other path seem very inviting, but do not fall for it! Keep in mind these questions are make-believe. How an actual fire fighter would respond in the field may not be the most appropriate way to convey your answer. Use the life safety order to help justify which path you have chosen and stick to it. When you presented with the situation, try to think of another way to accomplish the task; this will have to be a way that will keep you on the same path you have already picked but will show that you are not just giving up.

> Question: *"You just arrived at a house that is seventy-five percent involved in fire. With your training, you know the house is going to collapse. Are you going to go in?"*

If you choose to stay out of a burning building you know is going to collapse, you should use the life safety order to justify why.

> Path #1-

> Response: "I am not going into a house that is going to collapse because it is my safety first, my crew second, civilians, third and property, fourth."

> Board: "You look inside, and you see a woman trapped under a couch. Are you going in now?"

They are trying to get you to change your answer! **DON'T!** Remember, stick to your guns.

> Response: "I still have to say that I would not go in, but I would not give up. I would try to reach her with a pike pole or possibly a throw bag."

Again, stick to your guns. This is a horrible situation, but with the limited information given to you and the fact that it is make-believe, you need to stick to the path you chose. They will ask again to see if you will change your mind.

> Board: *You are unsuccessful with the throw bag and pike pole. Are you going in now?*

Response: *Unfortunately, I still have to say no. I did not cause the problem, but I will do everything within my power to help without risking my life. I need to think of how many lives I could save in the future. If I die here trying to save one life that is possibly already past saving, how many people could potentially die in the future? In addition, how many firefighters might get hurt or lose their lives trying to save me?*

For these compounding situational questions, sometimes it is better to step back and look at the whole picture. If you were to go in and the building collapsed on you, you did nothing to help the situation, and in fact, you made it worse. Other firefighters might lose their lives for you. If you died in this building trying to save something that was most likely already lost, what good have you done? Think of the lives you could save in the future if you were smart and looked at the whole picture.

Now let's look at the second path you could take.

Question: *You just arrived at a house that is 75% involved in fire. With your training, you know the house is going to collapse. Are you going to go in?*

Path #2

Response: I would make sure I heard the orders correctly and that my captain recognized the same dangers that I did. I am a new firefighter. It might look a lot worse to me than it actually is. I am charged with my crews' safety. I would go in with my experienced captain if he or she felt it is safe. I am equipped with top-of-the-line personal protective equipment and we have a Rapid Intervention Team in place.

As long as we perform and operate within the department's Standard Operating Guidelines, then I would go in.

Board: *You know the building will fall on you, are you still going in?*

Response: *In this department, we are a team. I am going to be there for my captain if it did collapse. One of us would be able to drag the other out. I feel safe because all the necessary safeguards are in place. If too much time is spent deciding what to do, then lives could be lost. Everything up until now has shown me that this captain to be level-headed and a great leader. I would go into any building that he ordered me.*

We have talked to people and the answers are mixed. We, the co-authors, have different opinions on which path we would choose. The bottom line is that it does not matter! Pick a path, stick to the path and justify why you chose that path. Choose the one you feel confident that you can defend.

Let's try another situational scenario.

Example #2

Question: *You are inside a building fighting a fire and running a low on air. Your captain tells you get two new air bottles. On your way to the engine, the Battalion Chief tells you to ladder the alpha-bravo corner of the building. What are you going to do?*

Path #1

Response: *I would let the Chief know that I am on an assignment to bring an air bottle to my captain. I am going to bring my captain air. I know my priority is my safety first and my crew's safety second.*

Board: *You are going to disregard the direct order from a Battalion Chief who has 30 years of experience?*

Response: *My priority is my safety first and my crew's second. I would go and get air for my captain and make sure he was safe. With my Captain safe, we could both go to ladder the building. With two of us, it might even be faster and safer than trying it by myself.*

The board will most likely come back with another reason why you should choose the other path. **Don't!!** Remember it is a game; if you switch you lose. Also, remember they have played this game many times before, and they are good at it. They will make the other path sound VERY appealing.

Path #2

Response: *I would let the Chief know that I am on an assignment to bring an air bottle for my captain. If the Chief still wanted me to ladder the building, I would ladder the building. I would radio my Captain to let him know I was on another assignment, and that I would be delayed getting him an air bottle.*

Board: *The radios are not working. Your Captain will not get the info.*

Response: *I would still ladder the building.*

Board: *You would leave your captain in there with low air?*

Response: *My captain is not trapped. The Battalion Chief has a lot of experience, is in charge of the entire scene, and knows my previous assignment. If he still feels that laddering the building is more important, then that is what I would do.*

Steer the answer:

*There might be a truck company in danger of a roof collapse or some trapped civilians that need help.*

Here again they will probably come back with something. Just stick to your path.


## Interpersonal

**Rule: Try to solve at the lowest level possible. If it does not get solved, then move up the chain of command.**

**Rule: Get all the information before addressing the problem.**

Your responses to interpersonal questions allow the interview board the opportunity to judge your ability to deal with conflict and to obtain a viable solution for the parties involved at the lowest supervisory level possible. Firefighters spend a great deal of time with each other under some extremely stressful situations. You will most likely be working 24-48 hours at a time with them, so being able to get along and resolve conflicts at the lowest level possible is paramount to operating as a successful team. It is important for the interview board to know you are capable of resolving conflicts professionally.

Take, for example, the question below.

Question: *You have noticed that a senior firefighter has not been completing his assigned chores, leaving you more work to accomplish on a continuing basis. This is frustrating since his apparent lazy attitude is adding significantly to your workload. How would you handle this situation?*

To address interpersonal conflicts, start at the source. In the example above, you should speak directly and professionally to the senior firefighter, express your concerns, and ask if there is a reason why he has not been able to get the chores done. Perhaps the senior firefighter is having difficulties in his personal life and small details such as housework are being forgotten. The first thing you need to find out is if there is really a problem, or if you are the one who is mistaken. It would be frustrating to create a confrontation if you simply looked at the housework list wrong, or if there was another list you did not see.

Be cognizant of word selection. For example, you should utilize the word *discuss*, instead of *confront*. You are attempting to convey to the interview board that you are assuming the positive. A harsh or condemning word such as *confront* will negate your positive outlook.

Now, think about the respect you'll earn if you address the problem privately and professionally (especially if there is an acceptable reason for the neglect), and the esteem you would lose if you handled a simple situation poorly. Remember, the last thing a busy Captain wants to hear is a complaint about somebody not taking out the trash, so aim to resolve it at the lowest level!

A word of caution, though. As with *Situational* questions, if the interview board offers enough information to prove your fellow firefighter is blatantly disregarding his duties, you must pursue the issue up the chain of command. If the issue is unethical or poses a threat to any person's safety, this must also be pursued up the chain of command, no matter how high you need to take it.

**Bizarre, Weird, or Just Different Questions**

Examples of Bizarre questions:

*How many cows are there in Canada?* - Google Interview

*If you were a pizza delivery person, how would you benefit from a pair of scissors?* - Apple Interview

Taken from: Website: staffsolutions.biz  "Top 20 Crazy Interview Questions by U.S.'s Greatest Companies"

These types of questions have become popular by various large non-fire companies. I have also heard of them being used by some fire departments during oral interviews. From the research we have completed, there is no right or wrong answer. The objective of these types of questions is to see how creative you are. We recommend trying to come up with something creative while incorporating the *TopScore Top Five*. The bottom line is to get creative and market yourself. There is a variety of examples of these types of questions throughout the internet so start coming up with some answers in your head so you are prepared for these peculiar questions.

## Core Values of a Firefighter

**Rule: Develop stories the board will remember.**

Question: *Why do people call 911?*

Answer - *They are faced with situations which exceed their abilities to cope. Firefighters face a huge variety of challenges. You will need a broad range of core values to succeed. Firefighting requires an individual to be able to think quickly on his or her feet and react promptly and correctly to situations which astound the normal citizen. On any given shift at the firehouse, you may be called on to use your strength and knowledge to forcefully open the door of a structure engulfed in flame, use your chemistry skills to determine how to take care of a hazardous material spill, utilize your mechanical skills to fix a broken fire pump, or tap into your interpersonal skills to console a grieving widow who has just witnessed her spouse pass from this world.* Get the picture?

The saying, "Jack of All Trades" has been used to describe firefighters. We disagree, for unlike the second portion of the saying, "Master of None," a firefighter must be a master of them all. There is no room for error; your fellow citizens depend on you.

We provide some of the Core Values we believe are essential to becoming a successful firefighter and that need to be woven into your *TopScore Top Five* answers. There are many important *Core Values,* and yours can be different, but do keep these in mind.

## Interpersonal Skills

Interpersonal skills are also known as social skills, people skills or emotional intelligence. These are life skills we use everyday to communicate and interact with people, both individually and in groups. People who have great interpersonal skills are naturally easy to get along with and can usually relate to those going through a stressful situation. Obviously, strong interpersonal skills in firefighters are a necessity to the fire service. Firefighters work as a team and interact with people on a daily basis in multiple settings. As a firefighter, you will be working closely with other firefighters in your department as well as residents within the community. It is important to maintain and grow these relationships to build trust and integrity. Although firefighters receive their paychecks from a fire department, we work for the citizens in the community. You should be willing to be approachable and eager to be involved in your community, anytime, anywhere.

I recently attended a family friend's 50th anniversary party. After the party ended, I offered to assist with cleaning up the plates and cups as well as vacuuming the floors and putting away the tables and chairs. I volunteered under the direction of an 80-year-old man who was the type of person that wanted things done his way. He had a particular process for clearing tables and putting the table and chairs away. Though it was clear there was a faster way, out of respect and patience, I followed his lead. Sure, it may have taken ten minutes longer than how I would have done it, but I was aware that he needed followers more than I wanted to fulfill my natural desire to lead. This would be an example of interpersonal skills.

You are with the same people for as much as 48 hours at a time when on duty at the firehouse. There will be times when your co-workers will get on your nerves. If your children (who you care so much about) can get under your skin, imagine how a middle-aged individual who snores and passes copious amounts of bodily gasses (and to whom you have no physical relations) could set you off! Interpersonal skills are things that you display on a daily basis, not just when on a call.

If you feel your Interpersonal Skills are lacking, *TopScore* recommends researching and reading books based on emotional intelligence. These books include emotional intelligence tests showing your strengths and weakness within your own interpersonal skills.

Think about where and when you have displayed positive interpersonal skills, and write a list of five times you have displayed unique interpersonal skills. Trust us; you have them even if you are a high school graduate who is just beginning to enter the workforce.

HOMEWORK

Interpersonal Skills That You Possess

1.

2.

3.

4.

5.

## Leadership

Leadership is the ability to positively influence others toward the achievement of a goal and is an important personality trait for firefighters. Leaders exude self-confidence (not arrogance) and respect the thoughts and opinions of others. Strong leadership fosters teamwork. An outstanding leader creates an atmosphere that inspires others to achieve their full potential. Leaders will have a vision of excellence that motivates and provides encouragement. A leader's demonstrated integrity creates a level of trust and confidence. Leading by example is the expectation of all firefighters, especially when interacting with the community.

The interview board is searching for leadership potential among the qualities of the applicants. Leadership is needed from Day One in the academy, and it continues throughout your career. At the fire academy, you will be surrounded by leaders. Obviously, not everyone can be the leader in all situations, but leadership attributes can still be demonstrated. The academy is challenging, and most of the material covered will be new to you and the other recruits. Studying and training outside of the classroom might be necessary. If so, someone should rally the troops and organize study and practice sessions. This person might as well be you.

Leadership in the field is important since the ranking leader might not be available. For example, truck companies could be staffed with four firefighters. When the truck company arrives, they split into two teams. In the absence of the captain, you must have the ability to assume leadership responsibilities when needed.

Every excellent leader has, at one point in time, needed to follow someone else's direction. It is no different in the fire service. Everyone must answer to someone in a position above him or her. The firefighter answers to the Captain, the Captain to the Battalion Chief (BC), the BC to the Fire Chief, the Fire Chief to the Mayor, and so on.

From the first day as a probationary rookie, you'll need to be a good follower. You'll need to follow Standard Operating Procedures, employee handbooks and direct instructions from your training captain and then from your crew. It is important to show the board how you have been successful as a follower in previous jobs and life experiences. At the same time, you need to express to the board your previous and current ability to lead.

Think about where and when you have displayed positive leadership skills, and write a list of five times you have displayed unique leadership skills.


HOMEWORK

How I've Demonstrated Leadership:


1.

2.

3.

4.

5.

## Teamwork

Every highly functioning fire department functions as a team. We encourage you to participate actively on teams with projects or on committees. Build respect from peers by contributing to the goals of the group. Model expected behaviors to accomplish team goals. Commit to the success of the group. Focus on the group's needs when taking actions. Act professionally and demonstrate flexibility. Always consider the impact of your actions on the group.

Everyone, and we mean **everyone**, has been part of a team. Teamwork should be one of the strongest points you will display.

Think about where and when you have exhibited outstanding teamwork in your own life and write a list of five times you have displayed this trait.

HOMEWORK

Ways I've Demonstrated Teamwork:

1.

2.

3.

4.

5.

## Communication Skills

Excellent communication skills require highly developed listening skills, as well as verbal and writing skills. The ability to articulate a point or make a verbal argument is crucial, as is the ability to concisely and properly make points in writing. You should listen actively and engage the person you are communicating with while utilizing open body language. Solicit feedback from peers and supervisors to create and expand upon self-development plans to increase your communication skills. The easy part of communicating is talking. The hardest and most important part is listening.

Most people, when they self-address their ability to communicate, default by thinking of times when they were able to effectively communicate the point they wanted to make. For me, one of the toughest communication components can be listening, and more importantly, listening to my shortcomings. I remember one of my first jobs as a young teen. I worked with a few friends on a landscape crew. It was a job outside under the sun and I was getting paid to hang out and visit with my friends who were also on the landscape crew. After two weeks on the job, I was called into the boss's office for my first evaluation. I walked into the meeting expecting a good report. I showed up to work early, worked as hard as or harder than most and never complained. He let me know the things I did well, which were music to my ears. He then said if I wanted to stay employed with him that I needed to eliminate the horsing around did while on the clock with my friends. He also said that, as a newer hire to the company, I needed to talk less and listen more. I remember saying to him that I would work on those things, but felt the pain of what I initially accepted as an insult to me. It was tough stuff to hear as a sixteen year old, but he was right. Sometimes being a good listener can be tough, especially if you feel you are getting your backend chewed. Bottom line, however, was that I was better for it. Listening has become a new priority for me whenever I am coached by someone who speaks of my shortcomings.

Think about where and when you have displayed positive communication skills, and write a list of five times you have showcased your communication skills.

HOMEWORK

Ways I've Displayed Affective Communication Skills:

1.

2.

3.

4.

5.

## Professional Development

Professional development is very important in the fire service. To develop professionally, you should:

- ✓ Act Professionally.
- ✓ Stay focused on the mission.
- ✓ Serve the customer.

- ✓ Treat everyone with respect.
- ✓ Display self-discipline.
- ✓ Demonstrate, model, and incorporate the tenets of trustworthiness, respect, responsibility, fairness, and caring.
- ✓ Learn, embrace, and market the department's vision statement and mission statement (usually available on the department's website).
- ✓ Show initiative and be self-directed.
- ✓ Pursue growth in every endeavor.
- ✓ Model a strong work ethic.
- ✓ Remain focused until a project is complete.
- ✓ Take responsibility for your actions.
  And...
- ✓ If you screw up, own it. Never Lie!!! Hold true to your word.

Professional development is continuous and is achieved in a variety of ways. This can be done with continuing education, seminars and podcasts, on the job experience and learning from and sharing with other firefighters.

Think about where and when you have improved or displayed positive professional development traits, and write a list of five times you have displayed this trait.

HOMEWORK

When/where I have demonstrated Professional Development traits:

1.

2.

3.

4.

5.


## Physical and Technical Expertise

This job requires you to be in great shape with a high level of cardiovascular fitness. Some Fire Departments require a mile-and-a-half run in less than 11 minutes, 30 seconds or employ other physical agility-based tests as part of entry-level testing. Begin a fitness program today. Your physical presence makes a strong impression to the oral board when you walk through the door. You need to show the board that not only you are fit for duty now, but that you will be fit for duty twenty-five years from now. No fire department wants to invest in a candidate not willing to commit to the level of fitness the fire service requires. Start now!

Think about your physical strengths and abilities and write a list of five times you have displayed this trait.

HOMEWORK

How I've Displayed Physical Traits and Abilities:

1.

2.

3.

4.

5.

## Innovation

Innovators are not afraid of change and are willing to consider a variety of alternatives. They possess the vision of where they would like to go and explore multiple options which allow them to reach their desired destinations. At the same time, innovators understand the various impacts of change and strive to think through options carefully before acting.

One of the best opportunities a supervisor can give a subordinate is to empower them to complete a given task. The supervisor describes how the result should look when complete. This gives the subordinate the freedom to be innovative in how the job is completed.

Think about where and when you have displayed innovative techniques and write a list of five times you have displayed this trait.

HOMEWORK

How I have Shown Innovation:

1.

2.

3.

4.

5.

## Diversity

People who truly value diversity understand the contributions made by persons of all nationalities, races, colors, sexual orientations and political and religious ideologies. They understand the useful role different opinions provide and are able to utilize skills in managing conflict while bringing about dynamic results. Diversity is broader than those categories protected by law and include differences which make us unique as human beings. These candidates are confident enough in their own beliefs to appreciate a different perspective or point of view.

Think about where and when you have embraced diversity in your own life (trust us, you have them) and write a list of five times you have displayed this trait. .

HOMEWORK

Ways I Have Shown Diversity:

1.

2.

3.

4.

5.

## Customer Service Skills

Firefighters with excellent customer service skills strive to ensure that customers are treated with respect and have a positive experience with the fire department. The needs of the customer take precedence over the needs of the person delivering the service. A person with these skills understands perception is as important as the service delivered.

An example good of Customer Service:

I worked for a local grocery store during high school, and my employer prided himself on the store's high level of superior customer service. It was on the first page of the employee handbook. I remember reading a particular paragraph. It stated, "If it is good for the customer and falls in line with the core values of the store, then it is a win-win."

One night, I was helping an elderly lady and bagging her groceries. When the job was done, I asked her if she minded me taking them out to her car. She replied that she lived behind the store in the mobile home park. She then said she would make a few trips walking back and forth from her cart she left by the front door of her house. I told her I wasn't going to let that happen and walked her cart and groceries to her front door. This was one of those specific incidents which the employee handbook did not cover other that the broad statement listed above. I did follow-up through the chain of command to my immediate supervisor, and he was pleased with the decision and said he would support that type of customer service any day.

Think about where and when you have exhibited superb customer service skills in your own life and write a list of five times you have displayed these traits.

HOMEWORK

Customer Service traits I have exhibited:

1.

2.

3.

4.

5.

## TopScore Marketing Priorities

**Rule: Blend your Marketing Priorities with the *TopScore Top Five* for the best possible answer.**

**Rule: Make sure you have perfected the *TopScore Top Five* before you start adding the Marketing Priorities.**

Polish. When you get to the point of being on your interview game, you will start to tailor your answers. Your answers will aligned with the greatest needs of the particular department in which you are interviewing. These are your *Marketing Priorities.* If the department takes pride in their members' level of fitness, then you, as a fit person, might have fitness as one of the marketing priorities to communicate in your interview.

For your *Marketing Priorities,* we want you to make a list of your top twenty-five attributes. These can be anything from a great sense of humor to a fierce loyalty to friends and family. This may seem like a large number, so brainstorm. Remember, there are no wrong ideas when you are brainstorming. Ask family and friends to assist you in this endeavor. Look at your Personal History from above. Examples might include your education, work history, and awards. Some of these may be extremely obvious and be listed on your resume. For example, maybe you worked as a wild land firefighter. This crucial piece of information needs to be presented to the oral board! More than likely, they know the dangers associated with a wild land fire, (if not, you are going to let them know) and can relate the changing winds and temperature of a forest fire to those of a structure fire. To top it off, they will understand you have probably been in some dangerous situations and reacted properly. If you have, write these down as well. Remember: brainstorm!). Your past needs to come out!

Once you have twenty-five items on your list, narrow it down to ten. Once again, utilize those closest to you to assist you in paring down the twenty-five to your top ten. You guessed it! These ten stories are your *TopScore Marketing Priorities*. They will be molded with the *Core Value* answers you listed previously and crafted into an answer utilizing the *TopScore Top Five* structure. It will take practice, but once mastered, you will speak flawlessly when sitting before the oral panel.

Rob's (one of the co-authors) ten marketing priorities prior to getting hired as a firefighter at age 25 in his own words:

> 1) *Hotshot Crew member. I worked for one of the United States premier Hotshot wild land firefighting crews. We, the team, worked in extremely hazardous environments, both physically and mentally arduous working conditions. We were expected to be in peak physical fitness at all times because we worked for days straight without sleep. During this job, it was my first real test with working in stressful conditions, and I was successful.*
>
> 2) *My values include being honest, being a man of integrity and exhibiting a great work ethic. The same ideals that this particular job announcement is seeking are the same ideals my parents raised me with since birth. My parents have always taught me the importance of respecting others as well as respecting myself, which has helped me fulfill my potential.*
>
> 3) *My high level of superior customer service. The fire service is in the business of providing customer service to its taxpayers. I was named Courtesy Clerk of the year in 1990,*

predominantly because of the level of customer service I demonstrated.

4) I am a dedicated teammate. Sports have been part of my life since I was six years old. I have played on teams that went undefeated as well as those who didn't win a single game. My memories of the years in which we finished last are not morose and regretful, but memories of the fun we all had playing together.

5) Dependable. I have always been described as being dependable. I think it goes back to what I was taught growing up regarding giving someone my word and sticking to it. If there is something that needs to be done, then I am your man.

6) I take pride in my work. I perform exceptional work and sign my name to it. I am not the kind of person who sacrifices speed for a shabby job.

7) Volunteer work. I enjoy volunteer work. One of my favorite jobs was volunteering during the winter (our seasonal off-time from the hotshot crew) at a local hospital. I answered phones and assisted with delivering flowers and balloons from the gift shop.

8) I am adaptable to any given changing situation. I grew up in a broken household. My parents divorced when I was 10, and this started a windfall of change. At age 14, I moved from California, where I was living with my mom, to Boise to live with my father. I had lived in the same town with my same friend my entire life, but despite that, I was able to

*meet and make friends almost immediately. I adapted to the changing situation, and moreover, I thrived.*

9) *My physical abilities. Being a firefighter requires a high level of both strength and cardio. I lift weights three days a week and either run or mountain bike the other days.*

10) *I am already a student of the trade. It is my ambition to be an exceptional professional firefighter. My desire and passion have me reading numerous firefighting publications and learning as much as I can. My brother, who is also a firefighter, shared that a firefighter will always be learning about the trade until his last day on the job.*

Here is an example of one of the most used Real interview questions.

Oral board: *Tell us about yourself.*

When practicing your interview, this is the polish you want to include in your *Marketing Priorities* (MP) and *Core Values* (CV).

Response: *My Name is Fred Gibbons. I grew up in a family of* (PH) *five on a (PH) tree farm where I learned (CV)(KW) work ethic, (KW)(CV) personal values and the (CV) importance of supporting those around you, just like you do here in the fire service. (PS) Some of my earliest childhood memories include my dad taking me by (DK) Station 1 and letting me climb on the trucks in my plastic firefighter helmet. As is (KW) tradition in the fire service and Backdraft Fire, (DK) the doors were always open, and my questions were answered with enthusiasm.*

I am currently a (MP)(PH) *paid reserve firefighter for a local Fire Department. I have earned both* (MP)(PH) *FF1 and* (MP)(PH) *EMT with them. I've always taken a personal interest in* (KW) *physical fitness. I'm an avid* (PH) *mountain biker,* (PH) *runner and rock climber, and I participated in* (PH) *high school sports.* (MP) *Events that I have participated in include multiple fundraiser* (PH) *stair climbs and a* (PH) *mountain bike race series in Oregon. I bring these up because it's an example of who I am and the lifestyle I live. These events allow me to stay* (KW)(MP) *active and involved with my* (KW) *community. I know how important volunteering is within the community. I have traveled and* (KW) *volunteered in some very* (KW) (MP) *diverse cultures. I also understand the* (DK) *importance of* (PH) *physical fitness and* (KW)(CV) *diversity to Backdraft Fire. I've had opportunities to speak with department members, and I understand the* (KW) *high physical standards expected during the* (DK) *recruit academy and throughout my career.* (DK) *These fitness standards include running, push-ups and sit-ups.* (DK) *I've seen Backdraft Firefighters' participation in the Seattle Stair Climb and other local events.*

*Additionally, I am not* (PH) *married. I currently work in the* (PH) *construction field as a* (PH) *framer, and at this time, I have yet to hammer a finger. I am very excited about this great opportunity to be interviewing with such a* (KW) *progressive fire department.*

## Oral Interview Wrap Up

*TopScore's Top Five* is the foundation for each *Real* answer; the *TopScore Marketing Priorities* interwoven with the *Core Values* are the polish used to ensure you've not only answered the question but have provided the oral board with enough information to really understand who you are and of what you are capable. Be thoroughly prepared for the board to close with a question such as "Is there anything you would like to add?" Look at it as an opportunity to let the board know about one or two of your marketing priorities that you might have missed. As a fellow interviewer stated, "I have never given a perfect score to an interviewee if this question was not answered." This is a valuable opportunity you need to exploit to your advantage!

During your closing remarks, you should briefly touch on each of the following items included below. Don't delve too deeply into these items; your response should simply be a concise summary of what you have discussed during the interview.

Summarize your qualifications.

Emphasize one of your best ten marketing priorities.

Reiterate how you would fit the department's values.

Illustrate how proud you will be to be a part of the department.

Thank them for their time and inform them you look forward to working with them in the future.

**Thank- You Card**

### Rule: Write a thank you card.

A thank -you card is one last opportunity to positively influence the interview board. To date, you've provided a professional resume and excelled at the interview by implementing the *TopScore* system. The interview board will take a copy of your resume to assist them while they determine the rank-order of the entire interview pool. Think of the thank you card as an opportunity to showcase your name and show how interested you are in becoming a member of their department.

Hand-write the thank you card. A handwritten card demonstrates a desire to go above and beyond what the average candidate would do. Let's face it, not many people hand-write letters these days. Anybody can sit down for a few seconds and fire off a clean-looking email with the use of grammar and spell check, but few are willing to take the time to hand-write a thank you card to each of the board members. Ensure that you mail them in time for the interviewers to receive soon after the interview. In fact, we suggest you write the cards immediately after the interview and mail them either the same day or the following at the latest.

You do not need to use this as an opportunity to remind the board members of why you would be a great hire. Your successful interview already answered that question.


Additional *TopScore* Rules for the Oral Interview

What may be apparent to some is not apparent to all. These simple rules will allow you to make a positive first impression on the oral board and gain their interest from the moment you walk into the room. Fail to follow these rules and you will significantly decrease your chances of gaining your badge before the interview has even begun. Some of these rules may be in the body of the book as well. It might be because they are important!

**Rule: You don't have a chance.** When you go for your ride-alongs, the crews will tell you they already know who they are going to hire. They are just trying to see if they can scare you off easy. Don't let it get to you. Just show them that if it is true, they are making a mistake.

**Rule: Be enthusiastic.** Nobody wants to spend 30 minutes listening to a hum-drum monotone voice. Have some enthusiasm and engage them.

**Rule: Smile as often as you can during the interview.** Smiling is contagious. It makes people feel good. When you smile, it also shows the board that you are enjoying yourself despite the stress the interview is causing.

**Rule: Dress to impress.** This is a job of professionals. You need to dress as such.

**Rule: Handshake.** Your handshake must be firm but not overpowering.

**Rule: Body language.** Your body language accounts for an enormous amount of what you communicate. Be engaging. Recording your mock interviews will allow you to assess and correct any issues with your body language. Take a neutral body position. Sit as if a string were connecting your head to the ceiling. Leaning back or slouching in the chair is seen as lazy or arrogant and leaning forward can be perceived as overly aggressive.

**Rule: Eye contact-** Strong eye contact shows confidence, and confidence is a sign of leadership. Eye contact should be made with each person on the oral board while you speak. Eye contact starts with the person who asks the question and from there, make eye contact with everyone else on the board, even if someone is ignoring you. Your answer should finish with your making eye contact with the person who initiated the question.

**Rule:  Be confident, not arrogant.** I have heard of people not being hired because they seemed too arrogant.

**Rule: The chair.** If your chair is 20 feet or more feet away from the board, ask if you can move it up. They will say," sure." Move it up to where you are closer, but don't lean on or touch the table.

**Rule: Lose the "ummmm"'s.** If they are counting your ummmm's you will probably not get hired. If you set the record, you definitely won't get hired! Record your mock interviews, count the number of times you use "ummm" and strive to eliminate them.

**Rule: The ignore.** One of the oral board members will not look at you. Ever! You must still try to make eye contact and try to engage him. This is part of the test.

**Rule: Positive statements.** If the oral board asks how you feel working with different types of people, ensure them you only think positively and answer accordingly.

**Rule: Never lie.** Don't lie or try to get one over on these guys. They are on the board because they are very good judges of character.

**Rule: Leave your cell phone in your car**, even if you have all of the stuff on there that you are trying to remember. It will look like you are posting on the internet.

**Rule: Do not chew gum.** This should go without saying, but it would not be here unless someone had done it.

**Rule: Do not interrupt anyone.**

**Rule: Show up thirty minutes early for your interview.** If they are ahead of schedule, your effort will be noticed and appreciated.

**Rule: Never include the following statements in your interview answer:**

> *The 20 days off a month will be great for me to have a second job.*

> *I am simply looking for a career change.*

> *I hope to get a few years of experience so I can go back to my home city and test.*

> *I am getting bored in my current job.*

**Rule: Bring enough resumes for everyone on the board to have plus a couple extra.**

**Rule: Social media.** There are many different types of background checks that Fire Departments conduct. Make sure your social media accounts are not offensive in any way.

**Rule: Prepare for a background investigation.** Get all of your background items collected before you need them. Some background checks are fifteen pages of information. You will only have one week to collect everything. If you have moved out of state from where you went to high school and college, this will make it difficult to acquire your transcripts in time. Do the work beforehand. This info will also be helpful in filling out your application. Some background checks can go back ten years or more.

**Rule: Application.** Get your application in first. Have someone proofread it, even if you are an English major and the world spelling bee champion four years in a row.

**Rule: Resume.** We recommend getting it done right the first time. There are classes or software if you do not want to pay a professional. Keep the resume to one page. We are professionals, but you are not applying to be the CEO of a major corporation.

**Rule: Thank-you letter.** A nice thank you letter is greatly appreciated. It also looks professional and gives you another chance for the department to see your name. Don't forget; it is a thank you letter, therefore, you are not going to talk about yourself.

## Keywords

**Rule: Use key words! They will notice!**

Below are keywords with which you should become familiar. These are examples, but do your research and find more. Find keywords meaningful to the department for which you are testing. These definitions are blended from *Meriam-Webster*'s, *Wikipedia* and *Dictionary.com* as well as TopScore preference when applied within the scope of the fire service.

**Pride -** a high or inordinate opinion of one's own dignity, importance, merit or superiority, whether as cherished in the mind or as displayed in bearing, conduct, etc.

**Respect -** Esteem for or a sense of the worth or excellence of a person; a personal quality or ability or something considered as a manifestation of a personal quality or ability.

**Integrity -** Consistency of actions, values, methods, measures and principles. Depth and breadth of a value system may also be significant factors due to their congruence with a wider range of observations. People have integrity to the extent that they behave according to the values, beliefs and principles they claim to hold. One's value system may evolve over time while retaining integrity if inconsistencies are accounted for and resolved. Hypocrisy results when one part of a value system is demonstrably at odds with another, and the person or group of people holding those values fails to account for the discrepancy. Hypocrisy is the opposite of integrity.

**Dedication -** A feeling of very strong support for or loyalty to someone or something.

**Excellence -** The state or quality of excelling, particularly in the field of business and organizations. Excellence is considered to be an important value and a goal to be pursued.

**Leadership -** The position or function of a leader, a person who guides or directs a group.

**Accountability -** In leadership roles, accountability is the acknowledgment and assumption of responsibility for actions, products, decisions and policies including the administration, governance and implementation within the scope of the role or employment position. This encompasses the obligation to report, explain, and be answerable for resulting consequences.

**Responsibility -** The state or fact of being responsible, answerable or accountable for something within one's power, control or management.

**Chain of Command -** A series of administrative or military ranks, positions, etc., in which each has direct authority over the one immediately below.

**Camaraderie -** A spirit of familiarity and trust existing between friends.

**Tolerance -** A fair, objective, and permissive attitude toward those whose opinions, practices, race, religion, nationality, etc., differ from one's own. Freedom from bigotry.

**Loyalty -** Faithful to one's oath, commitments or obligations.

**Fair -** Free from bias, dishonesty or injustice.

**Flexibility -** A personality trait; the extent to which a person can cope with changes in circumstances and think about problems and tasks in novel, creative ways. This trait is used when stressors or unexpected events occur, requiring a person to change his or her stance, outlook or commitment.

**Reliability -** Consistently good in quality or performance; able to be trusted.

**Honesty-** being able to be trusted for one's word.

**Motivation -** Interest in or enthusiasm for doing something.

**Positive Attitude -** Displaying a positive state of mind or feeling.

**Professionalism - :** The level of excellence or competence expected from a professional.

**Team Oriented -** Team oriented means you don't think of just yourself. You include others in your decisions. Everyone has a contributing factor in the operations and decisions.

**Trust -** Firm reliance on the integrity, ability or character of another person.

**Selfless Service -** Putting the needs of others before one's own.

**Compassion -** Deep awareness of the suffering of another coupled with the wish to relieve it.

**Attitude -** The manner in which someone carries oneself.

**Respect** - Showing admiration for someone based on his or her abilities, qualities or achievements.

**Responsibility/Accountability** - A form of trustworthiness; the trait of being answerable to someone for something or being responsible for one's conduct.

**Excellence** - A state of possessing good qualities to an eminent degree; exalted merit; superiority in virtue.

**Empowerment** - Knowledge of and faith in one's own ability.

**Humility** - Freedom from arrogance.

**Success** - The achievement of something desired, planned or attempted.

**Exceed:** To be better than. Go beyond what is expected.

**Mentor** - An influential counselor, coach or leader

**Comply** - To act accordingly; follow directions or a direct order

**Generate** - To cause to come about

**Excel** - Being exceptionally good and proficient in a subject or talent

## Sample Questions

Below are a series of sample questions with which to practice. Some might seem strange, but you need to find a way to relate them to the fire service using the *TopScore Top Five* system.

*Who is your favorite past President of the U.S. and why?* This is perfect for Key Words. Pick five good Keywords and match them with a president.

*What is the most important invention of all time, and why?* Use this one to demonstrate your department knowledge. Pick an invention and relate it to what you know about the department. Take, for example, the wheel. Talk about how the department benefits from the invention of the wheel. You can then transition to your department knowledge. You can start with the facts that there are six wheels on each apparatus. They have twenty engines, six trucks and a maintenance division to maintain the apparatus. Wheels are needed to respond to 30,000 calls per year with a ratio of 75 percent medical, 10 percent fire and 15 percent miscellaneous responses.

*Why is it important to be dependable?* Dependability is contagious; it shows dedication and it carries over. Dependability makes people passionate, and it makes people work hard for each other. It can be contagious within an organization. Being dependable fosters trust in your teammates, community and supervisors. It shows your dedication to obtain a goal and shows self-sacrifice.

*What word would best describe you?* Look at the department's mission statement and core values.

*What is the most appealing aspect of being a firefighter?* You will need to figure this out. Do not say anything like it will give me a lot of time to have a second job.

*How could you help maintain good relationships around the firehouse?* Be nice and show interest in your fellow firefighters families and hobbies.

*What are three characteristics of a good firefighter?* Look at the department's mission statement and core values let them know which ones you have?

*What type of person would you find most difficult to work with?* Think of safety.

*Define honesty and integrity and tell why they are important in the fire service.*

*What do you think about unions?* Talk to the union president. Look at the history of unions and why they started.

*What do you know about the organizational structure of the department?* Know that most departments have the following divisions: Administration Division, Operations Division, Training Division, Prevention Division and Logistics Division.

*Give some examples of how you provide customer service in your current job.*

*What is the primary goal of the fire department?* Think of customer service.

*What do you think of your previous boss?* Only positive statements.

*What motivates you?* Think of your *Key Words.*

*Give an example of when you worked with someone different than you.* Only positive.

*Would you ever disobey an order?* Yes, if it has to do with my safety or the safety of others.

*Define sexual harassment and give your feelings about the subject.* Think about this before your interview.

*What have you done to prepare for this position?* I like to think that everything I have done in life so far has helped me prepare for this position.

*What are you bringing to the job? Why would we select you over other candidates?* This is a good question for using department knowledge and key words.

*Why do you want to work for this agency?*

*What do you know about this agency?*

*What are your strengths?* Find out what their department values are. They could include customer service, fitness, tradition and many other things.

*What are your weaknesses?* Have a weakness that will not keep you from being hired, but you can show that you are working on and it is getting better. Do not have a weakness that is really a strength. The oral board will see right through it.

*What would your employer say about you?*

*Have you ever been in an emergency situation?*

*What word would best describe you?*

*What is the least appealing aspect of being a firefighter?*

*What do you think the future holds for the fire service?*

*Are you currently on any other eligibility lists?*

*What is the primary goal of the fire department?* Talk about the history of fire departments and why and who developed the fire service.

*When and how did you fail in a job or assignment?*

*What makes you think that you will be able to deal with the stress and strains of the job?*

How do you and your family feel about working 24-hour shifts?

*What is the advantage of working in teams?*

*What is the disadvantage of working in teams?*

How do you handle conflict?

Describe a time when you disagreed with a coworker?

Describe a time you were asked to do something wrong?

What is the toughest decision you have ever had to make?

What does leadership mean to you? Give examples.

Why is a healthy lifestyle important to the fire service?

What does integrity mean to you? How do you practice it?

What is your biggest mistake in life?

How do you evaluate success?

*Why are you leaving your current job?*

*What are the attributes of a firefighter? What is the most important to you?*

*What are three characteristics of a good firefighter? Which do you have?*

*Where do you see yourself in five years? Ten years?*

*Describe a difficult problem you had to overcome.*

*How would your friends describe you?*

*Who has inspired you in life?*

*What is the most appealing aspect of being a firefighter?*

*How would you handle racist/sexist comments?*

*Why do you want to be a firefighter?* You would be surprised how many people do not have an answer for this question.

*What if you suspect a fellow firefighter has a drug problem?*

*What if you see a fellow firefighter slip an expensive watch into his turnout coat during overhaul?*

*What if, during the final exam of your probationary academy, you see two fellow recruits exchanging answers?*

*What if your captain orders you to get him a radio from the engine and on the way, the Battalion Chief stops you and asks you to deliver an axe to the roof right away?*

*What if you feel a fellow firefighter is not pulling his or her weight?*

*What if you are assigned a task that you strongly feel is unsafe?*

*What if your shift Captain clearly delegates much more work to you than the other firefighters on the shift who happen to be his drinking buddies?*

## Resume

Your resume is an important piece of the interview process. After you leave a lasting impression on the interview board by implementing the *TopScore* system, your resume is the tangible piece they take with them. The application you filled out was most likely a single page, fill in the blank form that didn't allow much space for detail. The resume is an important marketing piece for you - treat it as such. Your resume should be kept to one page. Be sure to use high quality paper. A cover letter will not be needed. These are the general rules. If it states anything different in the job announcement, then, of course, follow the instructions.

Resume Template

name

address

email/phone

Objective- To become a firefighter in the City of Backdraft which will allow me the opportunity to use my fire suppression knowledge and skills to safely and confidently protect the citizens of this great city.

| | |
|---|---|
| Job- Summary | year-year |
| Job- Summary | year-year |
| Job- Summary | year-year |
| Job- Summary | year-year |
| Education- Summary | year-year |
| Education- Summary | year-year |
| Certificate | year |
| Certificate | year |
| Certificate | year |
| Hobbies | |

## Ride-Alongs

**Rule: When you show up, be part of the team.**

**Rule: Do The ride-alongs!!** A department ride-along is the perfect opportunity to learn about your prospective department and meet your future co-workers. Ride-alongs, in almost every agency, requires the filling out of at least some paperwork. That paperwork usually encompasses a liability waiver which needs to be signed.

**Rule: Wear appropriate clothing in layers.** You want to dress professionally but still be geared for a dynamic environment. Wear business casual with clean, closed-toe comfortable shoes. A collared polo shirt or button down shirt with khaki pants is appropriate. No hats. Bring a jacket if needed for the weather.

**Rule: Leave your phone in the car.** If you want to take some notes, use a pen and paper.

**Rule: Knock with your elbows.** This is an age old saying in the fire service. It has been the history in the service for a probationary firefighter to bring dessert when arriving for his first time at their assigned station. With their hands full, they had no other way to knock. We know you are not yet a probie, but play the part.

Remember, the station you are riding with is doing you the favor in providing you with an opportunity to come into their house as a guest. Show your appreciation by bringing a treat like a desert to share with the crew. For a nominal investment you can make a strong impression . You are basically thanking them for taking time out of their day to help you. It is not required, just recommended even though we call it a rule.

**Rule: Speak less and listen more.** Many people engaged in their first ride-along get quite excited. This leads to the motor mouth syndrome. It should go without saying that profanity and other unprofessional speech has no place in this environment. Remember: the ride-along serves as a layer of unofficial screening for the department. An old adage describing the fastest ways to spread news is "Telegraph, Telephone, or Tell a firefighter!" Word will travel fast if you wear your welcome out.

**Rule: Bring your own meal(s).** Plan on providing your own meals if you are riding during lunch or dinner. If the crews invite you to dine on what they are eating, try to pay your share. Sitting at the table will give you a personal and in-depth understanding of their world and their perspective, and it is another good time to speak less and listen more.

**Rule: Follow Instructions.** Follow the instructions of both the department and the host engine or truck company officer. This is a major responsibility for the agency and the officer; it's important to respect that.

**Rule: Jump in and help!** When crews are sweeping floors, washing the rigs or doing dishes, get involved and lend a hand. Stay away from the recliner and the T.V. During downtime, grab a firefighting magazine or book and sit at the kitchen table and learn something. Leave your cell phone in your car.

**Rule: Have your *TopScore* ride along questions ready.** This list does not include the answers to questions you can obtain on the department's website. Use this opportunity to ask questions which can only be answered through firefighters.

**Rule: Confidentiality.** Firefighters see a lot of interesting things in their line of work. Even Hollywood can't make up what firefighters see in real-life. As a participant in a ride-along, you may see neighbors and other people from your community at their worst moment. Specifics and identifiers from the call are not for public knowledge unless otherwise agreed upon. Adhere to all H.I.P.P.A. regulations as you will be held accountable to the same standards. Again, information being discussed is not public in nature, and you need to use discretion in discussing what you have seen and heard.

**Rule: Best Behavior.** Remember the entire time you are on your ride-along, you are going through an unofficial interview with members of the department. Shake hands with a "Thank You" to all members at the particular house.

**Rule: Ask questions.**

The following are sample questions you can address during your ride-along only if you were not able to find the answer through the Department's website: Remember that if you are asking questions in which answers are easily found on the internet, you are not showcasing your initiative.

The Basis for the following questions was given to me (Michael Zolin) by Michael Cisneros twenty years ago. Michael Cisneros was a Stockton Firefighter that mentored me for my first fire department interview. These questions are still relevant today, and with the advent of the internet it is much easier to find the answers. Like we said earlier it is good to have the information that can be found online, but much **better** to have information that **can't** be found online.

Who is the department Chief, and what is their history in the department?

Population?

Square miles?

How many stations?

How many engine companies?

How many truck companies?

Minimum manning?

Paramedics?

ISO rating?

Who is the Training Officer? Background?

Number of calls?

Call percentages? Fire/Medical/other?

Budget?

Who is the Fire Marshal?

Who is the Union President?

What is the fire loss per year?

What is the department budget?

What is the salary for each level of firefighter and what benefits are offered?

*What type of retirement is offered?*

*What is the department work schedule?*

*What is the training-drill frequency and what type of activities are covered?*

*What type of apparatus is located at the station?*

*Is there any special equipment at the station? e.g., Brush fire rigs or a riverboat?*

*What is the average response time?*

*How many battalions are in the department?*

*Are there any high-rise buildings in the district?*

*What is the pre-fire plan?*

*How many jobs are available?*

*Are there any unique hazards to the station? e.g., Refineries, lumber yards, chemical storage, rivers or highways.*

*What specialty teams are located at the station? e.g. Dive team or Hazmat.*

*What stations are the busiest?*

*What station is the best? Dog house?*

*Does the department use Incident Command? Blue Card?*

*What sports are played by the firefighters in the department?*

*What is the department history?*

*How many recruits fail the fire academy?*

*Who is the medical transport?*

*How long is the academy and what type of training can be anticipated?*

*What does an average day consist of?*

*For which nonprofit groups does the Union raise money?*

## Filling in Your Own Scorecard

Now that you understand the *TopScore* process and are capable of crafting quality answers using the system, you need to understand the six categories typically used to score an interviewing applicant. By understanding this, you will be able to indirectly fill out your own score sheet. The *TopScore Interview* scoring sheet is a measuring tool to see how well you perform in the interview setting. Knowing the categories that will be used to score your responses will help you prepare an outstanding *TopScore* answer.

One of the biggest challenges we have identified with those preparing for an interview is failing to recognize what the oral board is evaluating. For example, let's examine how one of our young daughters prepares for her gymnastics competitions, and more importantly, how she prepares to be judged.

Rob Christensen has a 6-year old daughter who understands that the gymnastic judges will award more points if her cartwheel is completed with straight legs. This item is important enough to warrant a specific block on the judge's score sheet. From the first day she learned a cartwheel, the importance of having straight legs was instilled in her mind. So much so that when she cartwheels around the house, she looks for feedback on the straightness of her legs. This same frame of mind needs to be engaged while preparing for your interview. You need to understand what is on the oral board's score sheet, and ensure you check every block for each question (A sample score sheet is provided later in the book). It should be your goal to make it effortless for the interviewer to award you the maximum score for your interview.

**TopScore Interview Score Sheet**

**Leadership**

Motivates others to take desired action or adopt attitudes having a positive effect on behavior: guides a group with common tasks or goals towards task/goal accomplishment; commands attention and respect, shows an air of confidence; originates action and attempts to influence events to achieve goals; sets task objectives and priorities and establishes a course of action for self and/or others to accomplish a specific goal.

| | |
|---|---|
| Excellent Leadership Skills | 90 to 100 |
| Good Leadership Skills | 80 to 90 |
| Acceptable Leadership Skills | 70 to 80 |
| Poor Leadership Skills | 60 to 70 |

## Interpersonal Sensitivity

Interacts with others to bring about desired attitudes; promotes cooperative relationships; is receptive to the suggestions of others; takes actions which indicates a consideration for the feelings and needs of others; shows an awareness of the impact that one's own behavior has on others.

| | |
|---|---|
| Excellent Interpersonal Skills | 90 to 100 |
| Good Interpersonal Skills | 80 to 90 |
| Acceptable Interpersonal Skills | 70 to 80 |
| Poor Interpersonal Skills | 60 to 70 |

## Cultural Diversity

Understands other cultures and cultural values and is confident in working with others of different backgrounds and diversity. Can identify with the feelings, thoughts and behaviors of individuals from different cultural backgrounds.

(A high score indicates that you are extremely capable of functioning in a culturally diverse workforce.)

| | |
|---|---|
| Excellent Culture Diversity Skills | 90 to 100 |
| Good Culture Diversity Skills | 80 to 90 |
| Acceptable Culture Diversity Skills | 70 to 80 |
| Poor Culture Diversity skills | 60 to 70 |

## Oral Communication

Orally conveys ideas or directives accurately, clearly and to the point; speaks smoothly and fluently, positively and enthusiastically; uses gestures, posture and eye contact with enhanced oral expression; is convincing and easy to understand; listens well to what others have to say.

| | |
|---|---|
| Excellent Oral Communication Skills | 90 to 100 |
| Good Oral Communication Skills | 80 to 90 |
| Acceptable Oral Communication Skills | 70 to 80 |
| Poor Communication Skills | 60 to 70 |

## Problem Solving and Reasoning

The ability to solve problems and make decisions is beneficial to the fire service because a high level of problem solving and reasoning saves firefighters from death and injury on a daily basis.

Problem solving is critical to the success as a firefighter because no two calls will be the same. Even similar emergency calls cannot be approached in the exact same manner. For example, two vehicle extractions could require entirely different extraction techniques and equipment. When answering your questions, it is important to demonstrate your capability to address a variety of problems and explain how your reasoning leads to a successful solution.

Ability to remember details and recall facts, to identify problems, recognize signs or symptoms of a larger or broader problem, plan an appropriate plan of action to reach an objective, develop alternative solutions and evaluate their relative value, to make sound decisions on the spot, etc.

| | |
|---|---|
| Excellent Reasoning/Problem Solving Skills | 90 to 100 |
| Good Reasoning/Problem Solving Skills | 80 to 90 |
| Acceptable Reasoning/Problem Solving Skills | 70 to 80 |
| Poor Reasoning/Problem Solving Skills | 60 to 70 |

**Mock Oral Interview Practice**

*TopScore* **Mock Interview Practice Scorecard**

Directions

This form is intended to be used by the person who is giving you a mock interview. The interviewer is to make note of the following: date, total time of the interview, time of each question answered, the interviewee's body language, fidgeting and "ums", eye contact and clarity of speech. The rating will be scaled from 1-10 with 10 being the top score. It is recommended that the practice session is videotaped.

Date_____          Interviewer(s)_____

Question_____?

Body Language_____    Speech_____    Eye Contact_____

Time_____


Did the question get answered?        Yes          No


Personal History          Yes          No          1 2 3 4 5


Personal Story            Yes          No          1 2 3 4 5


Department Knowledge      Yes          No          1 2 3 4 5


Key Words                 Yes          No          1 2 3 4 5

NOTES

_____

_____
_____
_____

_____

WWW.INTERVIEW911.COM

After learning the *TopScore* system, you must practice the implementation of the system. We are huge proponents of the mock oral interview. These mock interviews can be done with family or friends, or if you are in a position to know a firefighter, try to get it done at a fire station in front of firefighters. If practicing at a fire station, make sure you bring a peace offering for their time. Regardless of where your mock interview is done, you need to wear your suit and tie just as you will for your real interview. We recommend you do at least four mock oral interviews within two weeks of reading this book. This will allow you to become comfortable with the skills you've learned and hone your presentation by practicing in front of people. We also suggest you video record your mock interviews. Utilizing your cell phone will work perfect for this. This will provide you a frank assessment of your interview skills and will allow you to identify areas in the delivery of your response you can improve upon.

When reviewing your mock interview, count each non-verbal pause. Count how many times you fill a void in the conversation with unnecessary words such as "umm". Using "Umm," provides a chance for your brain to catch up with what you are trying to say. If you say "Umm" frequently, you need to find a way to stop. The board will not interrupt you because of a three second pause.

## Preparation timeline

When the test is announced, make sure you meet the qualifications and get in your application.

**Rule: 6 months prior:** or as soon as the test is announced:

Start doing research on the department. Review your resume. Gather all background information. Spend one hour per week on learning firefighting current events. Do one mock oral interview per month. Provide the interviewer of the mock interview with a list of *TopScore* common interview questions, and have them grade accordingly with the *TopScore Interview* score sheet. Do not take any timeouts if you stumble, learn to work yourself out of trouble. Do one casual interview per month. This can be done by yourself answering questions into a video recorder or with a friend or family member.

**Rule: 3 months prior:**

Do some ride-alongs with the department. Some departments may have a limit to how many you can do. Try to go to bigger stations. This will provide more practice! Start working in the information that you received from the ride-alongs into your answers.

**Rule: 1 month prior:** Department Knowledge!! Do a mock oral and casual interview.

**Rule: 1 week prior:** Make sure you have your closing statement dialed. Do two casual interviews and one last mock oral interview.

**Rule: No coffee the day of the interview:** You will be nervous enough the during the interview. There is no need to make it worse by drinking a bunch of coffee.

**Rule: 1 hr. prior:** Be there early!

**Rule: 2 min prior:** Power pose*! TopScore Top Five* confidence and enthusiasm, **You Got This!!**

**Rule: After the interview:**

> One of the best and fastest methods for capturing as much recall as you can is to utilize the voice recorder on your cell phone as soon as you can after the interview. Later on, you can listen to it so you can elaborate more in detail. At the very least, have a pen and paper to write down the information you remember from your interview.

**Rule: Immediately after your interview document the following:**

Names of members serving on the interview board.

All of the questions that you were asked.

Your response to the questions.

TopScore Top Five utilization.

What did you learn? From the board? About the process? About yourself?

What should you have done differently?

Send your thank you cards.

**Rule: Be passionate and stay committed.**

Take every opportunity to learn the things that can kill you and those who can keep you safe. With everything you learn, make sure it is shared with your brother and sister firefighters. There are many great websites and blogs that share fire training methods to help you learn. Thousands have been killed and or injured in this great profession. Please do not let those injuries and deaths go without bettering you and your crew. If this is a commitment you are not willing to make, please find another profession. We want our students to be leaders in the fire service for years to come. The fire service will be affected either positively or negatively by your being hired. It's up to you!

Congratulations! You are now one-step closer to achieving your goal. Now comes the hard part. Sorry, we have to say it again: practice. We now want you to write out your answers to all the real questions listed above. Do as we did and put (PH) (PS) (KW) (DK) before each corresponding word or story. Then count them. If you have met the requirements, most likely you have a complete and good sounding answer. After you feel you have the *TopScore Top Five* down, practice adding your *Core Values and Marketing Priorities*. Some people think that by writing out their answers they will sound canned. This is not the case. You will not be able to remember these answers word for word, but you will have a pool to draw from in order to come up with a great answer. Answer like one of our candidates did. When his interview was over, one of the board members looked to the others and said, "Does anyone else feel like standing up and clapping?" This is the response you are going for! We feel this book could be that boost you need for success on your next fire department interview. We also know the value of one-on-one personal coaching. With personal coaching, we are able to make sure you are implementing our system correctly and answer any questions you have on the testing process. Please visit our website at www.interview911.com

Thank you and good luck!!!

Made in the USA
Charleston, SC
12 May 2016